EMBLEMS *of* SOUTHERN VALOR

The Battle Flags of the Confederacy

FLAG OF THE SOUTH

Flag of the sunny Southland,
  Within your bonny folds
Are all the love, the hope, the dreams
  That the human heart e'er holds.

The love of sweetheart, wife, and home,
  Of honor, truth, and right;
Love of our sovereign right to live
  As God gave us the might.

In Memory of the Men Who Wore the Grey
by Anabel F. Thomason

Hope of the finest bravest men
  That 'e'er unsheathed a sword;
Knightly, true as steel were they -
  Men who sacred kept their word.

Dreams of our homeland unfulfilled,
  Bathed in the tears we shed -
Flag of sacrifice - symbol and shield
  Of our immortal dead.

EMBLEMS

of

SOUTHERN VALOR

THE BATTLE FLAGS OF THE CONFEDERACY

Joseph H. Crute, Jr.

Illustrations by Roland N. Stock

HARMONY HOUSE
Publishers Louisville

For my son, Hunter

Distribution by

OLDE SOLDIER BOOKS, INC.
18779 B North Frederick Avenue
Gaithersburg, Maryland 20879
(301) 963-2929
International Standard Book 1-56013-001-6
Library of Congress Catalog number 90-080981

Executive Editors: William Butler and William Strode
First Edition produced 1990 by Harmony House Publishers - Louisville
Box 90, Prospect, Kentucky 40059 (502) 228-2010/228-4446
Color Separations by Four Colour Imports, Louisville, Kentucky
Printed by Fetter Printing Company, Louisville, Kentucky

CONTENTS

$\mathcal{I}$NTRODUCTION

The Confederate flags carried during the War Between the States were symbols of the Southern people united in a common association. These symbols flew above a population of soldiers that were usually self-equipped and unpaid, were only marginally literate, and wore coarse, homespun jackets and trousers made by their mothers, wives and sisters. They were unique in character, self-reliant and independent, loyal to their commanders, but did not imitate "regular" soldiers. In the ranks were found men from every walk of life — lawyers, farmers, doctors, laborers, clerks, preachers, carpenters and dilettantes without any special calling. A large majority of them were opposed to secession, but as the inherent right of a state to secede from the United States was submitted to the arbitrament of the sword, they were compelled to serve their homeland.

The spirit of the Southern people created a determination to protect themselves from aggression, ambition, and conquest, and the flags of the Confederacy are proud relics of a cause for which thousands of valiant men fought and died.

For the most part their regimental battle flags are traceable to the Scottish Cross of St. Andrew, and in some cases to the English Cross of St. George. These flags not only promoted morale but played an important role on the field of battle. This was a black powder war and because of the clouds of smoke from musket and cannon fire, the waving colors were often the only visible point on which a commander could organize his troops. In the confusion of many voices, the sounds of bugle and drums and the harshness of enemy fire, many soldiers depended on a passing glance at the colors to identify nearby units. Also, the movement of flags could reveal the course and direction of a battle to an observant commander. Flags were often at the forefront of a successful attack; or a concentration of flags, such as those at Gettysburg on July 3, 1863, might indicate a defeat.

The tactical manuals adopted by both North and South provided that the colors be carried by a sergeant who was selected by his colonel. There was a color guard of several corporals posted around him, but any man or officer could carry the flag if the standard-bearer went down. The brave men who were entrusted with the colors lighted up the fields of Shiloh, Manassas, Chancellorsville, Gettysburg, Chickamauga, and countless others. Many official reports mention the courageous actions of the men who carried the battle flag. To keep the flag flying was a matter of extreme pride, and its loss to the enemy was always deeply regretted.

Understanding the close association between morale and colors, the Federals were known to concentrate a heavy fire upon Southern flag bearers. After the Battle of Sharpsburg General Paul J. Semmes wrote a report to Major James M. Goggin, A.A.G. on General McLaw's staff. He said: "In answer to the inquiry by Major-General Longstreet as to the number of colors lost by our troops in the battles in Maryland, I have the honor to state that no colors

Battle of New Berne - Lieutenant Hammond capturing Colonel Clark M. Avery of North Carolina

of Sergt. William N. Cameron, color-bearer of the Twenty-fifth Tennessee Regiment. In the last fight he advanced in front of his regiment so far that when it fell back he

were lost by the regiments of this brigade. In the Battle of Sharpsburg the colors of the Fifty-third Georgia received two shots; that of the Fifteenth Virginia, ten, and the pike was once cut in two; two color-bearers were wounded, and one of the color-guard was killed and one wounded. The colors of the Tenth Georgia received forty-six shots, and the pike was once hit and twice cut in two; one color-bearer and one of the color-guard were killed, and one color-bearer and one of the color-guard wounded . . ."

At Murfreesboro Colonel John C. Carter, 38th Tennessee Infantry, reported that Captain B.H. Holland died with the colors in his hands. Carter went on to say: "Color-Sergt. I.M. Rice was shot down. He still clung to the flag, and, crawling on his knees, carried it a short distance. Another bullet pierced his body, and death alone compelled him to yield to trust. A nobler soldier never lived, a braver never died." Also at Murfreesboro General Cleburne reported: "I wish to call particular attention to the gallant conduct

was unable to follow, and was captured. He tore the colors from his staff, concealed them upon his person, and made his escape from Bowling Green, bringing with him the flag of the Twenty-fifth Tennessee Regiment." At Corinth the flag of Lyles' (23rd Arkansas Infantry) Regiment was torn into tatters by the enemy's shots and color-bearer Herbert Sloane, when last seen by his comrades, was "going over the breastworks waving a piece over his head and shouting for the Southern Confederacy." Colonel Micah Jenkins, Palmetto South Carolina Regiment Sharpshooters, reported that at Seven Pines, ten of the eleven color guards were wounded or killed, and his colors passed through four hands without touching the ground. At Sharpsburg the 1st Texas Infantry lost eight standard-bearers and at Gettysburg the 26th North Carolina lost fourteen. Then at Appomattox the officers of the 11th North Carolina Regiment burned their flag rather than surrender it to the Federals. During the war hundreds of men died defending these flags, and hundreds more died trying to capture them.

When these flags were captured by the Federals, they were considered the property of the United States. Unless retained secretly by individuals, they were sent to Army Headquarters and usually forwarded to the War Department in Washington, D.C. The captors were given a 30-day furlough and awarded the Medal of Honor. The flags deposited in the War Department were exhibited at different times, then were placed in storage. On June 7, 1887, President Cleveland approved a War Deprtment order to return the flags. However, it was revoked by organized Federal veterans' groups. General Lucius Fairchild made his famous comment at a G.A.R. meeting denouncing Cleveland's order: "May God palsy the hand that wrote that order, may God palsy the brain that conceived it, and may God palsy the tongue that dictated it." So the Confederate flags remained in storage until 1905 when, during Theodore Roosevelt's administration, those that could be identified were returned to their respective States. The unidentified flags were given to the Confederate Memorial Literary Society (Museum of the Confederacy) in 1906. Since that time flags that were saved by Confederate soldiers have been donated to various Southern museums. Many are in private collections and many are still held by Northern States and museums.

National, State, company, and standard regimental colors were used in battle by Confederate forces. The purpose of this study is to present examples of the different surviving patters and some of the unique company designs. Many are tattered and torn, but these illustrations show the flags as they might have been carried. They are scattered throughout the country, and in preparing this study I have received assistance from several institutions and scores of persons. I particularly wish to express my thanks to Howard O. Hendricks, Rebecca Ansell Rose, and Guy R. Swanson, The Museum of the Confederacy, Richmond, Virginia; H. Michael Madaus, Milwaukee Public Museum, Milwaukee, Wisconsin; John M. Bigham, Confederate Relic Room and Museum, Columbia, South Carolina; William Long, the Old State House, an agency of the Department of Arkansas Heritage, Little Rock, Arkansas; Robert A. Serio, Prairie Grove Battlefield State Park, Prairie Grove, Arkansas; Mary Lohrenz and Jo Miles, Mississippi State Historical Museum, Jackson, Mississippi; Robert C. Peniston, Lee Chapel Museum, Washington and Lee University, Lexington, Virginia; June F. Cunningham, Virginia Military Institute Museum, Lexington, Virginia; Martha E. Battle, North Carolina Museum of History, Raleigh, North Carolina; Travis Hutchins, Georgia State Museum of Science and Industry, Atlanta, Georgia; Michael R. Green, Texas State Archives, Austin, Texas; Bill Pitts, Confederate Memorial Hall, Oklahoma

Historical Society, Oklahoma City, Oklahoma; Robert Cason, Alabama Department of Archives and History, Montgomery, Alabama; and the staff of the Virginia State Library, Richmond, Virginia. Also my thanks must go to Don Hillhouse, Epping, New Hampshire; Bill Turner, La Plata, Maryland; John McAden, Wilson, North Carolina; Lewis Leigh, Jr., Fairfax, Virginia; J. Carter Watts, Pine Bluff, Arkansas; and Lee Ware, Powhatan, Virginia.

Roland N. Stock of Richmond, Virginia, illustrated the flags and of course without his skill this book would not be possible. His illustrations include every known detail of the original flags. But remember, flag and unit information is irregular: some is complete and accurate and some is sketchy and questionable. For the reader who wishes additional information the bibliography at the end of this volume is suggested.

The war in Virginia. Beauregard's line defending Petersburg.

FIRST NATIONAL FLAGS

Flags are popular with most everyone; but in the career of secession the political, educational, and religious spirit of the Confederacy created a special interest in the proposition of a new banner. Even Raphael Semmes, Thomas R.R. Cobb, Alexander H. Stevens, Robert Toombs, William C. Wickham, and others took time out from their legislative and military duties to suggest new flag patterns. The Provisional Congress established a committee on February 9, 1861, to examine the many flag proposals. It was composed of Jackson Morton of Florida, Francis S. Barton of Georgia, Wiley P. Harris of Mississippi, John G. Shorter of Alabama, Edward Sparrow of Louisiana, and W. Porcher Miles of South Carolina, who served as its chairman.

The committee gave its report on March 5th. Some of the sentences from the original read: "Whatever attachments may be felt, from association, for stars and stripes (an attachment which your committee may be permitted to say they do not all share), it is manifest that, inaugurating a new government, we cannot, retain the flag of the government from which we have withdrawn, and any propriety, or without encountering very obvious practical difficulties. It is idle to talk of retaining the flag of the United States when we have voluntarily seceded from them . . . It must be admitted, however, that something was conceded by the committee to what seemed so strong and earnest desire to retain at least a suggestion of the old stars and stripes. So much for the mass of models and designs more or less copied from or assimilated to, the United States flag." The long report also states that the colonist forgot the British flag and wound up with this stand: "Yet under the British flag the colonist fought in their infancy for their very existence, against more than one determined foe. Under it they had repelled and driven back the relentless savage, and carried it farther and farther into the decreasing wilderness as the standard of civilization and religion. Under it the youthful Washington won his spurs in the memorable and unfortunate expedition of Braddock, and Americans helped to plant it on the Plains of Abraham when the immortal Wolfe fell. But our forefathers, when they separated themselves from Great Britian . . . they cast no lingering regretful looks behind." Then the committee commented on flags of other nations. "The committee, on examining the representations of the flags of all countries, found that Libera and the Sandwich Islands had flags so similar to that of the United States that it seemed an additional if not a conclusive reason why we should not 'keep,' copy, or imitate it. They (the committee) feel no inclination to borrow at second hand what had been pilfered and appropriated by a free negro community and a race of savages."

The committee went on to say, "A flag should be simple, readily made, and above all, capable of being made of bunting. It should be different from the flag of any other country, place or people. It should be significant. It should be readily distinguishable at a distance. The colors should be well contrasted and durable, and, lastly and not the least important point, it should be effective and handsome."

And summed it up: "The committee humbly thinks that the flag which they submit combines these requisites. It is easy to make. It is entirely different from any national flag. The three colors of which it is composed— red, white, and blue — are the true republican colors. In heraldry they are emblematic of the three great virtues, valor, purity, and truth . . .

W. Porcher Miles

emigrating to the United States. Smith's idea came from the Trinity, "The Three in One." He said the three bars stood for the state, the church, and the press. Red was for the state with its judiciary, legislative, and executive departments; white was for the church; red for the press with its freedom of speech; and all were bound together with the color blue. The seven white stars placed in a circle stood for the States, with equal rights regardless of size. The circle signified "You defend me and I'll protect you."

Your committee, therefore, recommends that the flag of the Confederate States of America shall consist of a red field with a white space extending horizontally through the center and equal in width to one-third the width of the flag, and red spaces above and below to be of the same width as the white, the union blue extending down through the white space and stopping at the lower red space, in the center of the union a circle of white stars corresponding in number with the States of the Confederacy."

By vote the flag of the Confederacy was adopted on the books of March 4th, to be of even date with Abraham Lincoln's inauguration. It was adopted with these words: "Long may this flag wave over a brave, a free and a virtuous people and may the career of the Confederacy be such as to endure this to our children, as a flag of the just government, the cherished symbol of its cherished truth."

Two men, Nicola Marschall of Alabama and Orren R. Smith of North Carolina, contributed to the design of the flag. Marschall stated he got his idea from the Austrian flag (three horizontal stripes of equal width, the upper and lower red, the center white) under which he served before

The flag with its seven stars (representing South Carolina, Mississippi, Florida, Alabama, Georgia, Louisiana, and Texas) was raised over the State Capitol at Montgomery, Alabama, on March 4th by Miss Letitia C. Tyler, a granddaughter of the tenth president of the United States, John Tyler. As more States joined the new government, additional stars were added to the flag. By the end of May, Virginia, Arkansas, Tennessee, and North Carolina were admitted to the Confederacy. Missouri and Kentucky became disputed territory, the Federal and Confederate Congress each receiving and welcoming delegations claiming to represent those States.

It was never adopted by Congress as the National Flag of the Confederacy. But news of the flag circulated throughout the South and it was soon flying over buildings and forts. Known as the "Stars and Bars," ladies began making the flag for hometown companies and regiments that were being organized. However, the stars in the union were not always set in a circle. Star design varied from flag to flag, and mottos, unit designations, and State seals were often incorporated in the blue union.

FIRST NATIONAL FLAG

CARRIED BY PORTERFIELD'S COMMAND

On June 3, 1861, the first land battle of the war took place at Philippi in western Virginia. Federal forces had been sent to the area to secure the Baltimore and Ohio Railroad between Washington and Parkersburg. They also wanted to recruit men for the Union army and clear all organized Confederate troops from Northwestern Virginia. Colonel George A. Porterfield was in command of about 750 Virginians who had been recruited during May in Upshur, Augusta, Highland, Bath, Pendleton, and Rockbridge counties. In the rain, Union General G.B. McClellan directed an early-morning surprise attack. The untrained Confederates, with their obsolete muskets, attempted to resist the Federals, but soon abandoned their position and equipment. During the conflict this flag was lost to the 16th Ohio Infantry Regiment. Later, on July 1st, Porterfield's command was mustered into Confederate service as the 25th Regiment Virginia Infantry. The flag is 49 inches by 103 inches, is made of cotton, and the lettering is painted. It is now in the collections of The Museum of the Confederacy.

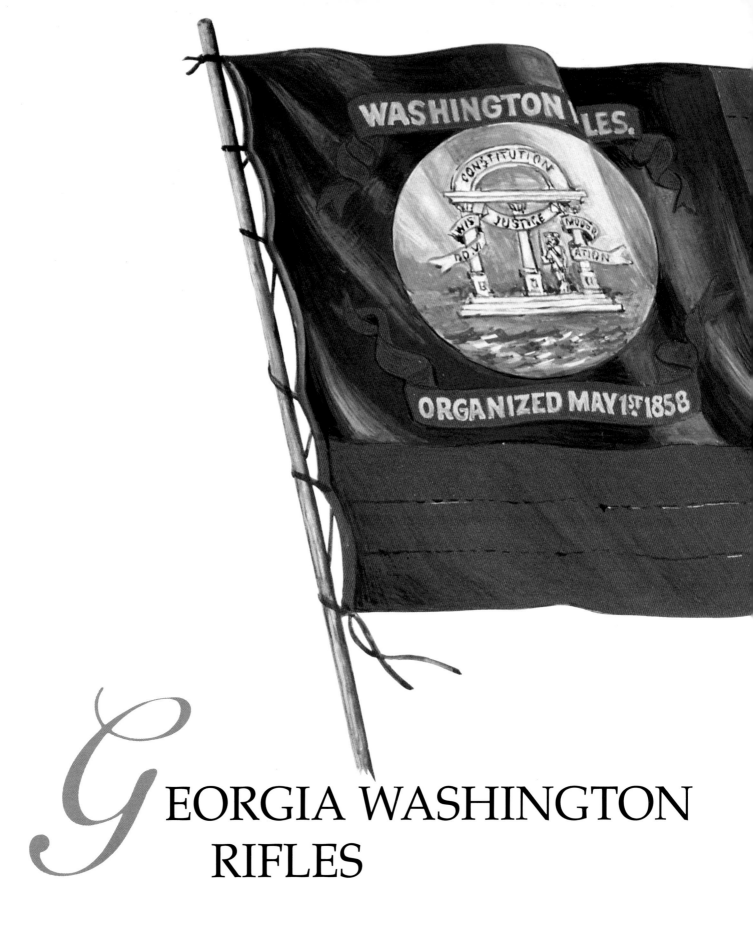

GEORGIA WASHINGTON RIFLES

Early in July, Ramsey's 1st Georgia Volunteers Infantry Regiment joined the Confederate forces in western Virginia. On the 13th day of July, General R.S. Garnett was killed fighting a rear guard action near Corrick's Ford on the Cheat River. He was the first general officer killed in the war. Also that day the Washington Rifles, Company E, 1st Georgia Volunteers, lost their colors to the

9th Indiana Regiment. The unit was badly shaken during this operation, but went on to serve in Lee's Cheat Mountain Campaign. In December, it was sent to Winchester, Lynchburg, and later Macon, where the regiment was mustered out of service. The silk colors of the Washington Rifles are now on display at the Georgia State Museum of Science and Industry. The Georgia State seal, adopted in 1799, is painted only on the obverse side of the flag. In the union on the reverse side are seven white stars set in a circle and red scrolls that read, "WE YIELD NOT TO/OUR COUNTRY'S FOES" in gold block letters. It measures 42 inches on the staff and 66 inches on the fly.

NORTH CAROLINA

Men of the Rutherford Volunteers were from Burke, McDowell, Mitchell, and Yancey counties and enlisted at Charlotte on May 28, 1861. They went into camp of instruction near Company Shops on June 1st and became Company E, 6th North Carolina Infantry Regiment State Troops. Ordered to Virginia, the unit fought under General B.E. Bee at First Manassas, then served in General Whiting's, Law's, Hoke's, Godwin's, and W.G. Lewis' Brigade, Army of Northern Virginia. It was prominent in the campaigns of the army from Seven Pines to Mine Run and at the Battles of Plymouth and Cold Harbor. Later the 6th participated in Early's Shenandoah Valley

RUTHERFORD VOLUNTEERS

operations and the Appomattox Campaign. It totalled 715 effectives in April, 1862, and surrendered six officers and 175 men of which only one sergeant and 11 privates were members of the Rutherford Volunteers. Their colors were retired early in the war. The star, wreath, mottos, and unit designation are painted on the silk flag which measures 39 inches on the staff and 81 inches on the fly. On the reverse side are painted fourteen gold stars surrounding a single gold star. The flag is now at the North Carolina Museum of History.

MARYLAND WINDER CAVALRY

The Winder Cavalry became Company E, 1st Maryland Cavalry Regiment during November, 1862. Their colors were presented to the company by the ladies of Kent County, Maryland, and shows the Maryland State seal adopted in 1854. On the reverse side set in a circle in the union are eleven stars and the motto "HOPE IS OUR WATCHWORD, TRUTH OUR GUIDING STAR." The flag was soon retired, but the eight-company regiment went on to fight in the Shenandoah Valley of Virginia, the Pennsylvania Campaign, and at Beaver Dam Station, Pollard's Farm, and Trevillian Station. It continued to serve in Early's Washington Campaign, McCausland's raid on Chambersburg, and around Appomattox. During the war it was active in numerous minor skirmishes and saw action in thirty-five engagements. The painted silk flag measures 27 1/2 inches by 46 1/2 inches and is at The Museum of the Confederacy.

MISSISSIPPI JEFFERSON DAVIS GUARDS

At the Mississippi State Historical Museum is a first national flag with an interesting star pattern. It was made by the Woodville, Mississippi Ladies Auxillary and presented to the Jefferson Davis Guards. The unit became Company D of the 21st Mississippi Infantry Regiment and was mustered into Confederate service on October 10, 1861, at Manassas, Virginia. It joined the Army of Northern Virginia and during the war served in General Griffith's, Barksdale's, and Humphrey's Brigade. The regiment saw action in the various campaigns of the army from the Seven Days' Battles to Gettyburg, then moved with Longstreet to fight at Chickamauga and Knoxville. After returning to Virginia it was involved in the Battles of The Wilderness, Spotsylvania, and Cold Harbor, Early's operations in the Shenandoah Valley, and the Appomattox Campaign. The company surrendered eight privates on April 9, 1865. Their colors were made of a wool fabric with cotton stars and measures 49 inches on the staff and 76 inches on the fly.

EIGHTEENTH REGIMENT VIRGINIA INFANTRY

On July 1, 1861, the 18th Virginia Regiment was accepted into Confederate service. It fought at First Manassas under General Cocke, then was assigned to General Pickett's, R.B. Garnett's, and Hunton's Brigade. The unit participated in the campaigns of the Army of Northern Virginia from Williamsburg to Gettysburg except when it was detached to Suffolk with Longstreet. Later it served in North Carolina, fought at Drewry's Bluff and Cold Harbor, and endured the hardships of the Petersburg trenches and the march to Appomattox. In the fight at Gettysburg, more than seventy-five percent of the 312 men in action were killed, wounded, or missing. The 18th lost its battle flag (St. Andrew's cross pattern) to the 59th New York Infantry, and presumably this flag was also captured at the same time, but proof is not available. Made of bunting and cotton with a silk fringe, it measures 42 inches by 55 inches. The flag is now part of the collections at The Museum of the Confederacy.

FIRST CHEROKEE MOUNTED RIFLES

The 1st Cherokee Rifles were organized at Old Fort Wayne, Delaware District, Cherokee Nation, in July 1861. It served in the Department of the Indian Territory and was later assigned to D.H. Cooper's and Stand Watie's Brigade, Trans-Mississippi Department. The regiment fought at Elkhorn Tavern; then, at Locust Grove on July 3, 1862, it sustained many casualties and lost its battle flag to a Federal force of Kansas and Indian troops. It continued the fight at Old Fort Wayne, Prairie Grove, Elk Creek, and Mazzard Prairie. About 200 officers and men saw action at Cabin Creek in September, 1864, but few surrendered on July 23, 1865. Their first national flag measures 49 inches by 79 inches, is made of cotton, and the stars are sewn on both sides. "CHEROKEE BRAVES" is painted only on the obverse side. The white stars represent the Confederate States; and red stars represent the Five Civilized Tribes (Cherokee, Seminole, Chickasaw, Creek, and Choctaw) that fought with the Confederacy. It is now part of a private collection.

COLONEL JOHN S. MOSBY'S PERSONAL FLAG

Mosby's Partisan Rangers, mustered into Confederate service as the 43rd Battalion Virginia Cavalry in June, 1863, served behind Federal lines in Loudoun, Fauquier, and Fairfax counties in Northern Virginia. The command was constantly on the move and never camped for very long in one place. The men were known for charging the enemy, believing that the shorter the time from start to finish the less danger there was. With a pair of Colt .44 revolvers, Mosby made himself as numerous and influential as possible. An infantryman captured in a charge was asked what made them break. "Why," he said, "you fellows came so quick we hadn't time to think, and besides, if we had shot the men off, the crazy horses would have run over us." The unit was the most effective command of its kind. Enemy forces were never safe and the area became known as "Mosby's Confederacy." After the Army of Northern Virginia laid down its arms, Mosby assembled his men at Salem, Virginia, on April 21, 1865, and said "Farewell." During the war his flag had limited use. It measures 51 inches by 114 inches, is made of bunting and cotton, and now rests at The Museum of the Confederacy.

GENERAL ROBERT E. LEE'S HEADQUARTERS FLAG

In May, 1865, General J.E. Johnston wrote to General J.M. Schofield, saying: "It has been reported to me that the archives of the War Department of the Confederate States are here (Charlotte, N.C.). As they will furnish valuable materials for history, I am anxious for their preservation, and doubt not that you are too. For that object I am ready to deliver them to the officer you may direct to receive them." Captain M.C. Runyan and his company (Company G, 9th New

Jersey Infantry Regiment) proceeded by rail to Charlotte and took possession of stores and a number of boxes containing the colors and battle flags captured from the Federal forces since the beginning of the war and the records of the War Department. In one of these boxes was General Robert E. Lee's headquarters flag. Its star pattern (Arch of the Covenant) is symbolic of the Bread of Life which is the symbol of spiritual nourishment. During her stay in Richmond, Mrs. Lee made small sewing kits (called a "Housewife") that showed a first national flag with the same star design. However, she omitted the two bottom stars. Late in the war these kits were given to friends as Christmas presents, and one that survives was received by John S. Mosby. Lee's flag was not used in battle, but was flown whenever he encamped for a period of time. It is made of bunting and cotton, measures 48 1/2 inches by 79 inches, and is now at The Museum of the Confederacy.

$\mathcal{T}$HE BATTLE FLAG

During the Battle of First Manassas, July 21, 1861, there was confusion identifying the combatants. Late in the afternoon, General Beauregard looked down the Warrenton Turnpike, which passed through the valley between the positions of the Confederates and the hill occupied by the Federals, and saw troops moving toward his left. The flags being carried hung close to their staff and because of the dust and smoke, it was difficult to determine if they were Federal or Confederate. Beauregard's anxiety was relieved when a breeze identified the "Stars and Bars." It turned out to be Colonel Jubal A. Early's Brigade which at that time was composed of the 7th Virginia, the 7th Louisiana, and the 13th Mississippi Regiments. Colonel Early also experienced some anxious moments and after the battle reported, " . . . I turned to the front and a body of the enemy soon appeared in front of my column on the crest of a hill deployed as skirmishers. Colonel Kemper's (7th Virginia) regiment, which was in advance, was formed in the open field in front of the enemy under a heavy shower of minie balls, and advanced toward the enemy. Colonel Barksdale's (13th Mississippi) and Colonel Hay's (7th Louisiana) regiments were sucessively [sic] formed towards the left,

and also advancd, thus outflanking the enemy. At the time that my brigade advanced the pieces of artillery (Beckham's Virginia Battery) . . . and Stuart's cavalry moved to our left, so as to command a view of a very large portion of the ground occupied by the enemy. With the advance of my brigade and the cavalry and artillery above mentioned the enemy retired rapidly behind the hill, though the advance of my brigade was delayed a short time by information from one of General Elzey's aides, who had gone to the top of the hill, that the body of men in front of us and who fired upon my brigade, was the Thirteenth Virginia Regiment. This turned out to be an entire misapprehension; and in the meantime a considerable body of the enemy appeared to the right of my position, on an extension of the same hill, bearing what I felt was the Confederate flag. It was soon, however, discovered to be a regiment of enemy forces, and was dispersed by one or two well directed fires from our artillery on the left."

Owing to the similarity of the "Stars and Bars" and the "Stars and Stripes," General Beauregard determined that Confederate soldiers should have a flag distinct in design and that a new flag for battle purposes must be created. He conferred

Hetty Cary

with Colonel W. Porcher Miles, who had served as chairman of the flag committee and was now V.A.D.C. on his staff, with the idea of securing such a flag. Miles suggested the pattern he had proposed for the national flag. While the design for a new flag was under consideration, many patterns were submitted and the matter discussed. When General Beauregard arrived at Fairfax Courthouse he directed his draughtsman, a German, to make drawings of all the various designs that had been proposed. The two favorite ones differed only to the shape of the cross, one bearing the St. Andrew's (Miles' recommendation) and the other the Latin (design submitted by Colonel James B. Walton, commander of the Louisiana Washington Artillery). He decided upon a red St. Andrew's cross upon a blue field with gold stars. Colonel Miles contended that the ground be red, the cross blue, and the stars white. Beauregard approved of the design and discussed it with Generals J.E. Johnston and G.W. Smith.

The design for the flag as submitted by Colonel Miles was rectangular in shape. Johnston modified it by making it square and prescribed different sizes for infantry, artillery, and cavalry. The officers at headquarters agreed upon a red field, a blue cross, and white stars, and the design was submitted to and approved in due course by the War Department.

Miss Connie (Constance) Cary and her two cousins, Miss Hetty Cary and Miss Jennie Cary, were entrusted in making the first three battle flags of the Confederacy. Connie was from Alexandria and Hetty and Jennie lived in Baltimore. Like many Baltimoreans, Hetty and Jennie had close ties with Virginia (they could claim Thomas Jefferson as a relative through both lines of the family) and their sympathies were with the South. Connie visited her cousins from time to time and in 1861 the temper of Baltimore was so strained that Federal troops were stationed throughout the city. But the Cary's and other friends of the "Monument Street Girls," defied Federal edicts.

Often styled the "Cary Invincibles," they wore the red and white Confederate colors in rosettes or in white aprons trimmed with red ribbons. The Federal soldiers were sensitive to these displays, and when Hetty waved the forbidden "Stars and Bars" in the face of troops marching past the Cary house, some of the junior officers sought to put her under arrest. One look settled the matter,

Jennie Cary

for the colonel in command said, "No, she's beautiful enough to do as she damned pleases."

No doubt as a result of Hetty's flag-waving, an order went out for her arrest. One of her brothers learned of the Federal action, and in the early summer of 1861 the two sisters made their escape to Southern Maryland. From there they crossed the lines to Virginia, carrying with them medical supplies. In Richmond, united again with Connie, they fitted into the circle of society that included Anges, Mildred, and Mary Custis Lee, Sally Corbett, Mary Triplett, Louise Haxall, the Davises, generals, and government officials. The Cary's set a style for entertaining with "Dutch treats" when guests brought their own food and the hostess supplied perhaps a ham and the tableware. Later their "starvation parties" featured lively dancing to piano music, but the refreshments were no stronger than water.

Work began on the flags as soon as they obtained a description of the adopted pattern. The making of these flags cannot be better described than in the words of Connie, who described the event in an article entitled "A Virginia Girl in the First Year of the War" published in *The Century Illustrated Monthly Magazine* (August, 1885). She said, "They were jaunty squares of scarlet crossed with dark blue, the cross bearing stars to indicate the number of seceding States. We set our best stitches upon them, edged them with golden fringes, and when they were finished dispatched one to Johnston, another to Beauregard, and the third to Gen. Earl Van Dorn, the latter afterwards a dashing cavalry leader, but he commanded infantry at Manassas. The banners were received with all the enthusiasm we could hope for; were toasted, feted, and cheered abundantly."

Probably as a gesture of gratitude, General Beauregard invited the three girls to visit the army encamped near Manassas. After dining in the general's tent, with Beauregard and his staff in attendence, they were serenaded by the Louisiana Washington Artillery band. When the concert ended and the soldiers called for a song from their guests, Jennie obliged with "Maryland, My Maryland." It was the first time the troops, including those from Maryland, heard the song. When the poem by James Ryder Randall was first printed on a "broadside" in Baltimore during May, 1861, the Cary's were taken by the sentiment of Randall's words and Jennie put them to music. She chose a popular college song, "Lauriger Horatius," based on the old German tune "Tannenbaum." The text, as first printed, had only the single word "Maryland" as a refrain: Jennie altered it to fit the music.

The girls had sent the flags to their favorite general. Hetty, having first choice, presented hers to General Joseph E. Johnston, then the lead-

Connie Cary

ing hero of the South; Jennie's went to General P.G.T. Beauregard, and Connie's to General Earl Van Dorn.

GENERAL VAN DORN'S FLAG

During January, 1862, Van Dorn was made commander of the Army of the West and subsequently transferred to the Army of the Mississippi. This flag was used in various conflicts including the Battles of Elkhorn Tavern, Corinth, and Holly Springs. After Van Dorn was assassinated in his headquarters by a Dr. Peters at Spring Hill, Tennessee, on May 7, 1863, Lieutenant Clement Sullivan of Maryland, General Van Dorn's nephew and A. D. C., returned the tattered and smoke-stained flag to Connie, in accordance with instructions found in Van Dorn's papers. On the reverse side is the name "Constance" embroidered on the lower arm of the cross near the hoist. The flag is 31 inches by 30 inches and the fringe measures three inches. It is now part of the collections of The Museum of the Confederacy. Beauregard's flag is privately owned and Johnston's flag seems to have been lost.

Soon after Van Dorn's flag was returned to Connie, she told this story: " . . . there arrived one day at our lodgings in Culpeper (Virginia) a huge bashful Mississippi scout, one of the most daring in the army, with the frame of Hercules and the face of a child. He was bidden to come here by his general, he said, to ask if I would not give him an order to fetch some cherished object from my dear home — something that would prove to me 'how much they thought of the maker of that flag'. After some hesitation, I acquiesced, although in jest. A week later I was the astonished recipient of a lamented piece of finery left 'within the lines,' a wrap of white and azure, brought to us by Dillon himself with a beaming face. He had gone through the Union pickets mounted on a load of firewood, and while peddling poultry had presented himself at our town house (in Alexandria), whence he carried off his prize in triumph with a letter in the folds telling us how our relatives left behind longed to be sharing the joys and sorrows of those at large in the Confederacy."

The three ladies were considered to be among the most handsome and accomplished of their day. Connie married Mr. Burton Harrison, aide to President Davis. After the war she traveled with her husband extensively and became a prolific novelist. Hetty was engaged to General John Pegram and the wedding on January 19, 1865, was one of the most billiant events in the last winter of the Confederacy. The bride's mother crossed the lines to be with her at the ceremony, and the sister of Mrs. Lincoln, returning South from a visit to Washington, took Hetty's trousseau along. As Hetty entered St. Paul's Church, her veil was accidently torn. Two days earlier she had broken a mirror. Within three weeks, February 6th, her husband was killed in action at Hatcher's Run. Jennie remained single and assisted her mother in the management of the Southern Home School for Girls on North Charles Street in Baltimore. She did not live long enough to see the poem she had set to music become the official song of the State of Maryland.

These flags became known as the "Southern Cross" and were the standard colors of the Army of Northern Virginia. Later, the Department of South Carolina, Georgia, and Florida, the Department of Alabama, Mississippi, and East Louisiana, the Army of Tennessee, and the Trans-Mississippi Department carried flags of the "Southern Cross" pattern.

SECOND NATIONAL FLAGS

Some of the Southern people had sentimental feelings for the "Stars and Bars" because it was similar in a general way to the flag of the United States. However, the Confederate struggle was for liberty and self-government, and as the war continued, their attitude reflected a change. On December 13, 1861, the *Daily Richmond Examiner* made this observation: "There is now little room for doubt that the resemblance of the Confederate flag to that of the United States renders it displeasing in the eyes of more than three-fourths of our population. . . the resemblance is so striking and essential that there is great difficulty in distinguishing the one from the other at a distance . . . Now, the very aim and object of a standard is to enable men and officers to know their own columns or ships from those of the enemy . . . A flag which cannot render that service is worse than none at all, for it may produce the most disastrous confusion and fatal errors. The desire for a change in the present banner has been so generally manifested that it is nearly certain that it will be made . . . If we change the present flag, the alteration must be final. Three things are de-

manded: First, that it shall be unique, so that it may be immediately distinguished from all others: Second, that it can be seen at great distance: Third, that it shall be handsome. To attain the first object, we must surrender the stars of every kind, and also give up red, white and blue, the colours of Imperial France as well as of the Lincoln despotism. To have the latter and most desirable quality, the colours must be as bright and as few as possible. A simple white flag, for instance, is seen by the naked eye at distances in which the figures of men and horse are imperceptible even with glasses. For the third deaideratum, no rule can be laid down save that the colours should be sufficiently broad as to fall in large masses. It will be difficult to create the standard that will meet these exigencies so long as we insist on preserving a tri-colour, and we are unable to perceive why it should be retained at all . . . we could have nothing better than a white ground, with the arms or emblem of the country, (whenever Congress shall find a committee of sufficient taste and knowledge of heraldry to make one) emblazed in gold or scarlet on the Union or in the centre."

Early in 1862, the people demanded a new national symbol that would not in any way resemble the Federal flag, that now stood for aggression and unjust persecution. Again the "Committee on a Proper Flag for the Confederate States of America" met to consider a new emblem. Many designs were submitted and on May 1, 1863, the "Stars and Bars" was replaced with the "Stainless Banner." The amendment read: "The Congress of the Confederate States of America do enact, that the flag of the Confederate States shall be as follows: The field to be white, the length double the width of the flag, with the union (now used as the Battle Flag) to be square of two-thirds the width of the flag, having the ground red; thereon a broad saltier of blue, bordered with white, and emblazoned with white mullets of five-pointed stars corresponding in number to that of the Confederate States."

General T. J. "Stonewall" Jackson

The new flag gave the Confederate States national identity, and was called the "Stainless Banner" because the solid white field was symbolic of the Southern cause. Unfortunately, the first flag made of this pattern was sent by President Davis to enfold General Thomas J. "Stonewall" Jackson's coffin as it lay in state in the House of Representatives at Richmond. Consequently, it is also called the "Jackson Flag."

As stated before, Confederate national flags were used in battle. After the second national flag was adopted, the Quartermaster Department in the eastern theatre issued several to various units serving in the Army of Northern Virginia. However, most units modified their flags by eliminating the white field which resulted in small battle flags. In the western theatre, no such flags were issued, but various groups did present them to particular battalions and regiments.

&IGHTH REGIMENT VIRGINIA CAVALRY

In the collections of The Museum of the Confederacy is the second national flag of the 8th Virginia Cavalry. This unit was organized in January, 1862, with nine companies but increased its number to 11 during July. It confronted the Federals in western Virginia, fought in East Tennessee, then returned to western Virginia. Later it participated in Early's Shenandoah Valley Campaign, including the conflicts at Fisher's Hill and Cedar Creek. The 8th moved to the Petersburg area and after the battle at Five Forks, served as rear guard for General Longstreet. It then cut through the Federal lines around Appomattox Courthouse and was probably one of the commands that disbanded on April 11, 1865, at Lynchburg. Their flag measures 53 inches on the hoist and 98 inches on the fly, is made of bunting and cotton, and the lettering and stars are embroidered.

ELEVENTH TENNESSEE INFANTRY REGIMENT

In the western theatre the 11th Tennessee Infantry Regiment is one of those units that adopted the second national flag as its regimental colors. The command was organized at Camp Cheatham, Tennessee, on July 1, 1861, and in July contained 880 officers and men. It skirmished in Kentucky, then saw action at Cumberland Gap and Tazewell. Later it joined the Army of Tennessee and served in General P. Smith's, Vaughan's, and Palmer's Brigade. The unit participated in the various campaigns of the army from Murfreesboro to Atlanta, fought with Hood in Tennessee, and was in the fight at Bentonville, North Carolina. It suffered 83 casualties at Murfreesboro, captured 200 prisoners and the colors of the 74th Pennsylvania Infantry Regiment at Chickamauga, and totalled 340 men and 267 arms in December, 1863. After the Atlanta Campaign, it was consolidated with the 29th Tennessee Regiment and was included in the surrender on April 26, 1865. The colors of the 11th Infantry are made of silk and the unit designation and battle honors are painted. It measures 33 1/2 inches by 67 inches and is now in the collections of the Tennessee State Museum at Nashville.

GENERAL JUBAL EARLY'S HEADQUARTERS FLAG

Second national flags were also used at the headquarters of several general officers. They usually measured four feet on the staff and six feet on the fly and were made of bunting and cotton. General Early's flag was lost March 2, 1865, at the Battle of Waynesborough, Virginia. It was captured by the 22nd New York Cavalry Regiment which was one of the units under the command of General George A. Custer. The flag was returned to the State of Virginia on April 26, 1905, by the U.S. War Department and is now at The Museum of the Confederacy. It measures 47 inches by 72 1/2 inches.

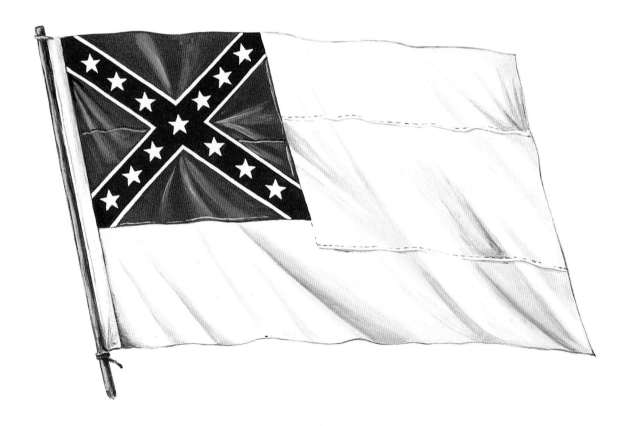

GENERAL "JEB" STUART'S HEADQUARTERS FLAG

J.E.B. Stuart's bravery, professionalism, endurance, and good humor made him one of the great cavalry leaders in America. His command fought at First Manassas, Williamsburg, and in the Seven Days' Battles when on July 25, 1862, as Major General, he took command of all the cavalry in the Army of Northern Virginia. Stuart's cavalry went on to participate in the battles at Second Manassas, Fredericksburg, Chancellorsville, Gettysburg, The Wilderness, and Spotsylvania. On May 11, 1864, he was mortally wounded at Yellow Tavern and died the following day in Richmond at the home of his brother-in-law, Dr. Charles Brewer. His flag was made by his wife, Flora. It was never used in actual combat but whenever General Stuart encamped, he ordered a tall sapling cut to which this flag was attached and placed over his tent. Made of bunting and cotton, it measures 46 inches by 74 inches and is part of the collections of The Museum of the Confederacy.

$\mathcal{T}$HIRD NATIONAL FLAGS

Because of its too liberal white, the second national flag proved unsatisfactory. It could be mistaken as a flag of truce or surrender and naval officers stated that it was too similar to the English white ensign. This led to new suggestions and again the *Daily Richmond Examiner* commented: "Before we get our national emblem we must get rid of stars and stripes in all their variations. So too of all arrangments of red, white and blue . . . The national emblem of the equestrian South is the horse. Its colors are black and white; its shield is the sable horse of Manassas on a silver field; its flag is the white flag with the black horse. Neither belong to any other nation of Christians." This proposal met with some approval especially because of the incorporation of the horse, but was rejected. Objections to the second national flag were reviewed by a Military Committee, and on March 4, 1865 the Confederate States of America adopted its third national flag with this resolution: "The Congress of the Confederate States of America do enact, that the Flag of the Confederate States shall be as follows: The width, two thirds of its length, with the union (now used as the Battle Flag) to be in width three-fifths of the width of the flag, and so proportioned as to leave the length of the field on the side of the union twice the width of the field below it; to have the ground red and a broad, blue saltier thereon, bordered with white and emblazoned with mullets or five-pointed stars, corresponding in number to that of the Confederate States; the field to be white except the other half from the union to be a red bar extending the width of the flag."

The flag was designed by Major Arthur L. Rogers, an artillery officer. He stated that the heraldic significance of the predominately white and red colors are especially appropriate for the Confederate States, the white being emblematic of purity and innocence and the red of fortitude and courage. Rogers went on to say that the people of the South are chiefly descended from the British and the French, and the cross of St. Andrews was from the former and the red bar from the flag of the latter nation.

Very few third national flags survived because only a small number were made and carried in battle. Most that did were second national flags that were modified.

GEORGIA UPSON COUNTY GUARDS

During the spring of 1865 the Upson County Guards of the Georgia militia were stationed near Macon. On April 20th, the 17th Indiana Mounted Infantry was forty-five miles from the city. After a twenty-four mile march, the 17th met a small force of Confederates at Spring Hill. There was another conflict at Montpelier Springs and then at Tobesofkee Creek at Mimm's Mills. When the Federal unit reached Culloden, one and a half miles from Macon, there was a sharp skirmish and the flag of the Worrill Greys, also of the Georgia militia, was captured. The flag of the Upson County Guards was probably also captured in this action. The 17th captured five flags that day, but only four were turned in to the War Department. This flag was retained by its captor and subsequently became part of the collections of the Chicago Historical Society. Their records indicate that the flag was made in England by some titled ladies in 1864 as the "Stainless Banner" and was later modified after the adoption of the third national flag. It measures 42 1/2 inches by 88 1/2 inches, is made of bunting and cotton, but its cross and stars are silk.

STATE FLAGS

The South had not even thought of a flag under which to fight until at Harper's Ferry, when the militia captured John Brown, someone asked, "Under what flag shall we fight?" The noted Turner Ashby grasped the flag of Virginia and said, "I am going to fight under this." By the end of September, 1861, many of the Confederate States had adopted State flags to show their independence.

When Alabama seceded on January 11, 1861, a magnificent flag was unfurled. On one side was a representation of the Goddess of Liberty, holding in her right hand a sword unsheathed, and in the left a small flag with one star. In an arch just above this figure are the words, "Alabama Independent Now and Forever." On the reverse, the prominent figure is a cotton plant with a rattlesnake coiled at its roots. Immediately above the snake are the words "Noli Me Tangere" which translates "Touch Me Not." Also on the same side appears the Alabama Coat-of-Arms. The *Montgomery Advertiser* of January 12th carried this editorial: "Yesterday will form a memorable epoch in the history of Alabama. On that day our gallant little state resumed her sovereignty, and became free and independent . . . the beautiful flag, presented by the ladies of the Convention, was run up on the Capitol, the gun squad began to fire a salute . . . the various church bells commenced ringing and shout after shout might have been heard all along the principal streets." The figures were painted in natural colors on a dark blue field. But as beautiful as this flag was, few were made and none were carried in battle.

During the Constitutional Convention of 1787 it was agreed that each State, while loyal to the United States Flag, should also have its own flag. In 1799 Georgia selected a blue flag with its Coat-of-Arms in the center. This seal was described as having the Arch of the Constitution supported by three pillors of Justice, Wisdom, and Moderation. When Georgia seceded on January 19, 1861, a modified version of this flag was presented. It is questionable that any were ever used in battle because no Georgia Flag of the size carried in combat survived the war.

Turner Ashby

The flag adopted by Florida on September 12, 1861, modified the "Stars and Bars" by extending the blue union the width of the flag. In the center of the blue bar was incorporated a new seal that shows an oak tree growing near the Gulf of Mexico with ships in the background. Under the tree is a cannon, cannon balls, a stand of arms, a drum, and crossed Confederate and Florida flags. Surrounding the scene was the inscription 'IN GOD IS OUR TRUST" and "FLORIDA." The colors of Florida were never used in battle.

Neither Arkansas, Missouri, Kentucky, or Tennessee enacted legislation for new flags. However, Tennessee did propose a flag that would replace the stars in the union of the first national flag with the seal of Tennessee. A few units did carry such a flag, but the Tennessee seal was also placed on company flags. And as shown in this study, other states, such as Georgia, incorporated state seals in the union of the first national flag. Today there exist only three State flags, Virginia, South Carolina, and Texas, that were flown during the war.

LOUISIANA STATE FLAG

UNIDENTIFIED

The Bonnie Blue Flag (blue field with a single white star) had been used by the Louisiana Florida parishes when they formed the Republic of West Florida in 1810. Also the brown pelican was the symbol of Louisiana for many years. However, when Louisiana seceded, the people wanted a new symbol to proclaim their independence from the United States. On February 11, 1861, a flag was adopted that contained thirteen horizontal stripes like the Federal flag, but used the Bonnie Blue pattern for the union. The new flag incorporated the blue, white, and red of France and the yellow and red colors of Spain because both countries had been prominent in Louisiana's history. During the war some Louisiana troops did carry a blue flag with a white star and some used the pelican on their banners. This unidentified Louisiana State flag was also used in battle. Although it lacks a unit designation, the flag is definitely a unit flag because of its metallic wire fringe. Made of silk, it measures 47 1/2 inches on the hoist and 71 inches on the fly and is now at the Texas State Archives at Austin.

SECOND REGIMENT VIRGINIA INFANTRY

Virginia seceded on April 17, 1861. Also that month, the 2nd Regiment Virginia Infantry was organized at Charles Town, (then) Virginia, and at Harper's Ferry was placed in T. J. Jackson's Brigade. The unit soon moved to Winchester, and on July 18th was ordered to join Beauregard's forces at Manassas Junction. As the regiment passed through Winchester it was presented this flag. It was made by George Ruskell Manufacturers of Richmond, and the presentation was made under the sponsorship of Miss Virginia Rutherford of Charles Town. At the First Battle of Manassas, July 21st, this was the only Virginia flag carried into battle by Jackson's command. The South Carolina troops, stationed immediately in the rear, at one time broke and started to withdraw from the field. It was then that General B.E. Bee rallied them with the cry: "Look! There is Jackson, standing like a stone wall! Rally behind the Virginians!" This was the christening of the brigade which was ever afterwards to the known as the "Stonewall Brigade." It was composed of the 2nd, 4th, 5th, 27th and 33rd Regiments of Virginia Infantry.

On the reverse side of the 2nd Regiment's flag is the Virginia State seal which was adopted during the Revolution. Its moto translates "Thus Ever to Tyrants." After the fight at Manassas the flag was returned to Miss Rutherford for safekeeping. She stated, "It was brought to her by a little bare-footed colored girl, who wound her way among Federal troops encamped on the grounds surrounding our home. Carrying a small package wrapped in newspaper, she came to a side door and handed the package to a member of the family saying, 'Give this to Miss Ginny Rutherford,' and darted away." No one ever learned who the little girl was or who gave her the flag. Miss Rutherford's father wrapped the flag carefully and put it and other family treasures under an iron hearth in a bedroom. There it remained until after the war. The hand-painted silk flag of the 2nd Virginia measures 40 inches on the staff and 58 inches on the fly and is now on display at the Virginia Military Institute Museum.

EIGHTH NORTH CAROLINA INFANTRY REGIMENT STATE TROOPS

The 8th North Carolina Regiment was organized at Camp Macon, near Warrenton, North Carolina, during September 1861. It was soon ordered to Roanoke Island and the men set up camp near Fort Bartow and worked on the fortifications. Toward the end of the year, General A.E. Burnside planned an expedition against the coastal installations in North Carolina. The enemy fleet entered Pamlico Sound at Hatteras Inlet and attacked the island on February 7, 1862. The next day the island was surrendered and the State flag of the 8th was lost to the 24th Massachusetts Infantry Regiment. On the reverse side of the flag, which was adopted on June 22, 1861, the vertical red bar contains two dates; May 20, 1775, for North Carolina's independence from Great Britain, and May 20, 1861, for her independence from the United States. The letters and figures are painted in gold on gold-edged green scrolls and between the dates is a six-pointed silver star edged in black, all of which is framed in elaborate gold. The silk flag measures 39 inches by 62 inches and is now in a private collection.

FIRST SOUTH CAROLINA REGIMENT RIFLES

South Carolina adopted its State flag on January 28, 1861, and in February ladies throughout the State presented the flags to units being organized. It was a blue flag that contained a white palmetto tree and white crescent. On July 19th, the 1st South Carolina Regiment Rifles, known as Orr's Rifles, was assembled at Sandy Springs. It moved to Sullivan's Island and on October 4th in front of the Moultrie House was presented this flag by Colonel Isaac W. Hayne of Charleston. After Colonel J.L. Orr received the flag he extended his thanks and made one of his best speeches. Then, turning to the ensign, he said, "Sergeant (R.H.Y.) Lowry, I know this flag will never trail the dust till its folds cover your body." The flag was made by Mrs. Alexander H. Mazyck and Mrs. Ellison Capers and was attached to a staff taken from a nullification banner of 1832. It measures 26 1/2 inches by 46 inches, and on the reverse side is the Confederate first national design with eleven stars set in a circle. The white stars, crescent, and palmetto tree were made from a white silk dress belonging to Mrs. Mazyck and the blue ground from a silk dress of Mrs. Capers. The unit designation and date were painted. The regiment soon left for Virginia and joined the Army of Northern Virginia. Their colors were retired early in the war and are now at the Confederate Relic Room and Museum, Columbia, South Carolina.

FIRST TEXAS INFANTRY REGIMENT

Texas adopted a flag on January 25, 1839 that showed the lone star of the Republic on a vertical blue bar and two horizontal bars of white over red. It is still in use today. During the spring of 1861 this flag was made and presented to the 1st Texas Infantry Regiment by Miss Lula Wigfall, daughter of its colonel, Louis T. Wigfall. In August the unit moved to Richmond, Virginia, and later carried its State flag in the Battles of Seven Pines, Gaines' Mill, Malvern Hill, and Sharpsburg. Here it lost eighty-two percent of the 226 men engaged and its colors to the 9th Pennsylvania Regiment. Lieutenant Colonel P.A. Work, who commanded the regiment during the battle, wrote in his report, "It is a source of mortification to state that, upon retiring from this engagement, our colors were not brought off . . . the loss of our flag will always remain a matter of sore and deep regret." Eight men were shot down trying to protect the flag. As part of Hood's Texas Brigade the 1st went on to fight at Fredericksburg, Gettysburg, Chickamauga, Knoxville, and in the Petersburg trenches. It surrendered at Appomattox with 16 officers and 133 men. Their flag measures 56 inches by 55 1/2 inches, is made of silk, and the battle honors were painted. It is now part of the collections of the Texas State Archives at Austin.

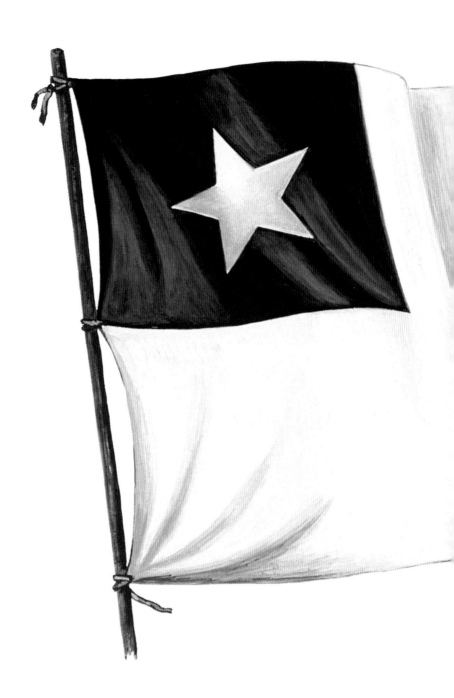

THIRD MISSISSIPPI
INFANTRY REGIMENT

On January 26, 1861, Mississippi adopted an official State flag to proclaim her independence. It incorporated The Bonnie Blue Flag with a magnolia tree on a white field and red fringe along the fly edge. This flag was used in battle, but its maker and history of capture is unknown. Along the bottom are painted gold letters, outlined in blue, that read: "THE BLUE FIELD WITH THE WHITE STAR, THE MAGNOLIA LEAVES, RAGGED BORDER AND FRINGE ARE ALL THAT REMAIN OF THE OLD FLAG OF THE 3D REGT. MISS. VOLS. RESTORED BY THE VETERANS OF THE 9TH REG. CONN. VOLS. FEB 26, 1885." The 3rd Infantry was organized at Enterprise, Mississippi, during the spring of 1861. It fought in and around Vicksburg, then served with the Army of Tennessee during the Atlanta Campaign and in Tennessee and North Carolina. It totalled 572 men in February, 1863, but had only 71 present for duty during December, 1864. The flag measures 51 inches on the staff and 74 inches on the fly, is made of silk with a wool fringe, and the tree is painted. It is now at the Mississippi State Historical Museum.

COMPANY FLAGS

Early in the conflict, as units were being assembled, local women created unique flags because they were thought to be essential to organization. Many were about five or six feet long and were made of silk or homespun cotton. In most cases a unit designation or motto was applied to the flag and some were beautiful works of art. Painted on the flags were scenes of home, State seals, or State symbols such as the palmetto tree of South Carolina or the Louisiana brown pelican. A great number of these flags were of the first national pattern, covered earlier in this book. The flags presented in this chapter were of original design.

When the work was completed, the flag typically would be presented to a company with flowery remarks. For example, Miss Ldelea Collens offered the colors to the Desoto Rifles, which later became Company D, 5th Louisiana Regiment. The *New Orleans Daily Crescent* on April 29, 1861, reported her remarks: "Receive them, from your mothers and sisters, from those whose affections greet you, these colors woven by our feeble

but reliant hands; and when this bright flag shall float before you on the battlefield, let it not only inspire you with the brave and patriotic ambition of a soldier aspiring to his own and his country's honor and glory, but also may it be a sign that cherished ones appeal to you to save them from a fanatical and heartless foe." Then the Color-Sergeant responded: "Ladies, with high-beating hearts and pulses throbbing with emotion, we receive from your hands this beautiful flag, the proud emblem of our young republic ... To those who may return from the field of battle bearing this flag in triumph, though perhaps tattered and torn, this incident will always prove a cheering recollection and to him whose fate it may be to die a soldier's death, this moment brought before his fading view will recall your kind and sympathetic words, he will . . . bless you as his spirit takes its aerial flight . . . May God of battles look down upon us as we register a soldier's vow that no stain shall ever be found upon thy sacred folds, save the blood of those who attack thee or those who fall in thy defense. Comrades you have heard the pledge, may it ever guide and guard you on the tented field, or in the smoke, glare, and din of battle, amidst carnage and death, there let its bright folds inspire you with new strength, nerve your arms, and steel your hearts to deeds of strength and valor."

Captain James J. White

About the same time, April and May, 1861, a company of mostly college students from Washington College (Washington and Lee University) was being organized at Lexington, Virginia. The ladies of Rockbridge County formed a sewing society that provided uniforms for the men. Muskets and caps secured from the Virginia Military Institute were emblazoned with brass letters of the company's initials, "L.H.V." (Liberty Hall Volunteers). On June 8th, the unit marched to the courthouse on Main Street. Captain James J. White's command was indeed a handsome group. Each volunteer wore a white waist belt and cross belts fastened with a big brass buckle over his gray uniform. His ankles and calves gleaming in white gaiters and his head adorned with a snowy havelock, Rev. John Miller delivered an eloquent speech and presented a beautiful flag, made by the ladies of the Falling Springs Presbyterian Church, to the company. It was inscribed with the words "Pro aris et focis" which translate "For altar and home." After a prayer by the Rev. Dr. W.S. White, the college boys departed for Staunton, then Winchester, where they became Company I of the 4th Regiment Virginia Infantry.

After the First Battle of Manassas Confederate officers realized that it was dangerous for every company to fly its own colors. Many of the early company flags were returned home for safekeeping after a few engagements and were generally replaced by standard regimental battle flags.

FLORIDA INDEPENDENT BLUES

Organized on July 15, 1854, the Florida Independent Blues entered Confederate service on August 10, 1861, as Company B, 3rd Florida Infantry Regiment. The men were recruited in Jefferson County and the unit was also called the Jefferson Beauregards or the St. Augustine Blues. This flag was presented to Captain J. Lott Phillips' Company by the ladies of St. Augustine. It was made by Miss Emma Westcott who was assisted by Miss Anna Dummett, Miss Mary Louise Dunham, Mrs. M.D. (Dunham) Taylor, Mrs. M.L. Abbott, Miss Lucy Abbott, Mrs. Judge Smith (mother of General E. Kirby Smith), Mrs. Cooper Gibbs, and Mrs. Laura C. Gibbs. The ribbons in the upper left corner identify the company and give the date of organization. In the center of each star is the date of the first seven States that joined the Confederacy. The regiment served at Mobile, fought at Perryville, then during December, 1862, was consolidated with the 1st Florida Infantry Regiment. This command went on to fight in various battles from Murfreesboro to Bentonville and surrendered with the Army of Tennessee. The ribbons, stars, half-blown cotton bole, and motto were sewn on the flag. It was made of cotton and silk, measures 45 inches by 70 inches, and is now on display at The Museum of the Confederacy.

VIRGINIA RAPPAHANNOCK CAVALRY

The Rappahannock Cavalry, often called The Old Guard, was organized at Washington, Virginia, on April 22, 1861. It was presented this flag by a group of Gordonsville ladies when it passed through the town on the way to join T.J. Jackson in the Shenandoah Valley. The flag was first flown in battle on May 23rd when the company charged the enemy off the Winchester-Front Royal Pike near Cedarville. Of the 38 men only three came out of the clash still mounted and unharmed. There were 10 killed and 14 wounded and the eighteen-year-old color bearer was pierced by twenty-one bullets. The unit became Company B of the 6th Regiment Virginia Cavalry during September and later served under Generals Robertson, W.E. Jones, Lomax, and Payne, Army of Northern Virginia. Only three men of the 6th Cavalry surrendered at Appomattox as most of the cavalry cut through the Federal lines and disbanded. The cotton flag was retired early in the war and measures 25 inches by 47 inches. It is now at The Museum of the Confederacy.

ALABAMA PEROTE GUARDS

During March, 1861, the Perote Guards of Bullock County became Compay G, 1st Alabama Infantry Regiment. The unit moved to Missouri, and in the fight at Island No. 10 the company and its colors were captured on April 7, 1862, by the 15th Wisconsin Regiment. In the union on the reverse side is a painted seal of Alabama in full color. As to the motto "JUSTICE & PROTECTION to each new partner or a new firm," Colonel Hans Heg of the 15th Wisconsin stated: "This rather mystical legend is doubtless to express, that in the opinion of the Perote Guards each new state should be devoted to niggers [sic] or the Union must be desolved, indicating that they were conditional Union men ." After being exchanged, the 1st was sent to Port Hudson. Here it was again captured on July 9, 1863. Exchanged and reorganized, the regiment fought in the Atlanta and Tennessee Campaigns and ended the war in North Carolina. The silk flag measures 52 inches on the staff and 90 inches on the fly and the stars, motto, and unit designation are painted. It is now at the Alabama Department of Archives and History at Montgomery.

LOUISIANA PELICAN RIFLES

The Pelican Rifles, also called the De Soto Creoles, became Company K of the 3rd Louisiana Infantry Regiment during the spring of 1861. The unit fought at Wilson's Creek and Elkhorn Tavern, then moved to Mississippi where it was active at Iuka and Corinth. Later it was assigned to General L. Herbert's Brigade in the Department of Mississippi and East Louisiana and was captured in the fight at Vicksburg. After being exchanged, the regiment served in General A. Thomas' Brigade, Trans-Mississippi Department. The company's flag is made of silk and on the reverse side is the motto "SOUTHERN RIGHTS INVIOLATE" surrounded by a wreath of laurel and oak leaves, all of which is painted in gold. At the top of the wreath, "PELICAN RIFLES" is painted in gold on a dark blue scroll and at the bottom is a purple bow. It measures 61 inches on the staff and 59 inches on the fly. The flag was lost to a Wisconsin unit, but information on its capture is not on record. It was returned to the State of Louisiana in 1943 and is now at the Louisiana State Museum in New Orleans.

NORTH CAROLINA KENNEDY LIGHT ARTILLERY

This company was raised in Beaufort County by Reverend Charles P. Jones, who became captain. After a few months of service, the battery was reorganized by electing Z.T. Adams, captain. It was assigned to the 13th North Carolina Artillery Battalion as Company D, but the battalion did not serve as one command. The Kennedy Light Artillery was attached to the Department of North Carolina and Southern Virginia, saw action at Washington and New Bern, then in 1864, was stationed at Kinston. Later, it was at Batteries Purdie and Bolles near Fort Fisher and on January 15, 1865, most of the company and all its guns and horses were captured. The few remaining men were attached to General Hagood's Brigade, fought at Bentonville as artillerymen, and surrendered with the Army of Tennessee. Their silk flag was never lost or surrendered and measures 46 inches on the staff and 43 inches on the fly. It is now part of the collections of the North Carolina Museum of History at Raleigh.

TENNESSEE LEBANON GREYS

The women of Lebanon, Wilson County, Tennessee, presented this flag to Captain John K. Howard's Company, the Lebanon Greys. It moved to Camp Trousdale in Sumner County and on May 28, 1861, became Company H of the 7th Tennessee Infantry Regiment. Ordered to Virginia, the unit saw action in Lee's Cheat Mountain Campaign, and for a time served under General T.J. Jackson. Later it was assigned to General S.R. Anderson's, Hatton's, Archer's, and McComb's Brigade, Army of Northern Virginia. The 7th fought with the army from Seven Pines to Cold Harbor, endured the long Petersburg siege, and ended the war at Appomattox. It sustained 72 casualties during the Seven Days' Battles, 38 at Fredericksburg, and 56 at Chancellorsville. Of the 249 engaged at Gettysburg, forty-six percent were disabled. Only 6 officers and 41 men surrendered, of which two sergeants and five privates were from the Lebanon Greys. Their colors were retired after standard regimental flags were issued to the army. The seal and inscriptions were painted on the silk flag that measures 58 inches on the hoist and 90 inches on the fly. It is now in the collections of the Tennessee State Museum at Nashville.

VIRGINIA PRINCESS ANNE CAVALRY

On April 20, 1861, men from Princess Anne County, Virginia, enlisted to serve the Confederacy. A cavalry company was formed and after some reorganizations, Captain Edward W. Capps' command was assigned to the 15th Regiment Virginia Cavalry as Company C. The unit served in General W.H.F. Lee's, Lomax's, and Payne's Brigade, Army of Northern Virginia, and took an active part in the Chancellorsville, Bristoe, Mine Run, and The Wilderness campaigns. After the fight at Cold Harbor, it moved with Early to the Shenandoah Valley, then on November 8, 1864, was absorbed by the 5th Virginia Cavalry. The company's silk flag was made by The Ladies Aide Society of the London Bridge Baptist Church, was hand-painted on both sides, and measures 34 inches on the staff and 35 1/2 inches on the fly. Never lost or surrendered, the colors of The Princess Anne Cavalry are at The Museum of the Confederacy in Richmond.

SOUTH CAROLINA WILLIAMS GUARDS

At Williams, Colleton County, South Carolina, a Mrs. Trezevant presented this flag to the company in May, 1861. The unit moved to Columbia and became Company B, 3rd South Carolina Infantry Regiment. Ordered to Virginia, it saw action at First Manassas in Bonham's Brigade, then served under Generals Kershaw, Kennedy, and Conner, Army of Northern Virginia. The regiment totalled 550 effectives in April, 1862, lost 135 at Savage's Station, 49 at Maryland Heights, 84 at Sharpsburg, and 163 at Fredericksburg. Of the 406 engaged at Gettysburg, twenty-one percent were disabled. It continued the fight at Chickamauga, Knoxville, The Wilderness, Spotsylvania, Cold Harbor, and with Early in the Shenandoah Valley. The 3rd moved to North Carolina and after the Battle of Bentonville, had a force of 191 officers and men. Never lost or surrendered, the hand-painted silk flag of the Williams Guards measures 40 inches on the staff and 42 on the fly and is at the Confederate Relic Room and Museum, Columbia, South Carolina.

$\mathcal{M}$ISSISSIPPI BURT RIFLES

With men from Hinds County, Captain E.R. Burt's Company was organized during April, 1861. Later, the Burt Rifles moved to Corinth and joined the 18th Mississippi Infantry Regiment as Company K. On June 7th, Captain Burt was commissioned colonel of the regiment. Ordered to Virginia, it fought at First Manassas under D.R. Jones, then was engaged at Leesburg. Here the unit suffered 85 casualties and Colonel Burt was mortally wounded. The 18th then served in General Griffith's, Barksdale's, and Humphrey's Brigade, Army of Northern Virginia. It took an active part in many campaigns from the Seven Days' Battles to Cold Harbor, including the conflicts at Chickamauga and Knoxville, and participated in Early's Shenandoah Valley operations. The company surrendered at Appomattox on April 9, 1865, with one second lieutenant, one corporal, and one private. Their hand-painted silk flag was never captured or surrendered. It measures 42 inches on the staff and 43 inches on the fly and is at the Mississippi State Historical Museum at Jackson.

BEDFORD'S KENTUCKY CAVALRY

With men recruited in central Kentucky, the 5th Cavalry Regiment was organized during the summer of 1862 and Captain James G. Bedford's command became Company C. The regiment was attached to General A. Buford's Brigade which was involved in various skirmishes in Tennessee and Kentucky. This flag was presented to Captain Bedford by Mrs. Maggie Brent McCoy and was carried by the unit when it confronted the Federals in Nelson County, Kentucky. Here Bedford was wounded and the flag was torn from its staff and used as a bandage. Later, a surgeon gave the flag to Mrs. Bedford. The unit went on to fight with J.H. Morgan and most of its members were captured at Buffington Island and New Lisbon, Ohio, during July, 1863. The regiment was not reorganized. The cross and stars, representing their belief that their cause was justified by religion and patriotism, was sewn on the silk flag. On the reverse side is sewn the motto "ON TO VICTORY" in large white letters. It measures 36 inches on the staff and 42 inches on the fly and is now in the collections of The Museum of the Confederacy.

MISSISSIPPI WAYNE RIFLES

The Wayne Rifles were organized at Waynesboro, Wayne County, Mississippi, during April, 1861. This hand-painted silk flag, made by Mrs. Miller and Mrs. Echford, was presented to the company of which W.J. Echford was captain. Its motto translates "Protector and Avenger." With about 80 officers and men, the unit marched to Corinth and during May became Company C, 13th Mississippi Infantry Regiment. The colors were carried by Theodore Shaw at First Manassas, then his brother, John Shaw, carried the flag in several other engagements. William C. Pou was the color bearer at Malvern Hill and was shot down still holding the flag-staff. The company flag was later returned to Waynesboro and for many years kept in the Courthouse. After serving in the campaigns and battles of the Army of Northern Virginia, The Wayne Rifles surrendered at Appomattox with no officers and 6 men. Its battle flag measures 47 inches on the staff and 62 inches on the fly and is now at the Mississippi State Historical Museum at Jackson.

GUIBOR'S MISSOURI BATTERY

Captain Henry Guibor's artillery company was organized with men from the Missouri State Guard in February, 1862. After fighting at Elkhorn Tavern, the unit was ordered east of the Mississippi River and during January, 1863, was presented this flag by some patriotic ladies of St. Louis. It was carried by the company until the siege of Vicksburg when it was given to a Mr. Gennelli for safekeeping. The unit was captured on July 3, 1863, and after being exchanged served in G. S. Storrs' Battalion of Artillery, Army of Tennessee. It saw action in the Atlanta Campaign and Hood's Tennessee operations, but in 1865 the small command disbanded. After the war, Guibor reclaimed the battery's emblem. Now at The Museum of the Confederacy it measures 45 inches by 55 inches and the unit designation and battle honors are painted on the silk flag.

ARKANSAS JEFFERSON GUARDS

The Jefferson Guards were organized at Pine Bluff, Jefferson County, Arkansas, and entered Confederate service on April 27, 1861. During May, Miss Etta Bocage, the seventeen year old daugher of Judge J.W. Bocage, made and presented this flag to Captain Charles Carlton who commanded the company. During this time the Guards had joined Cleburne's 1st Regiment, but later became Company B of the 15th (Cleburne's—Polk's—Josey's) Arkansas Infantry Regiment. After the Battle of Murfreesboro, when more uniform regimental flags were issued, Captain Carlton folded away the colors of the Jefferson Guards. Carlton was later captured by cavalry troops from Illinois and it seems likely that the flag was also captured at that time. It is made of silk and the motto "FIAT JUSTICIA RUAT COELUM" is the Latin phrase, "LET JUSTICE BE DONE THOUGH THE HEAVENS FALL." On the reverse side are fifteen gold stars surounding a cotton plant in natural colors and in gold letters the motto "Regnant Populi" which translates "The People Rule." The flag measures 49 inches by 95 1/2 inches and is now on display in the Courthouse at Pine Bluff.

SOUTH CAROLINA KING'S MOUNTAIN GUARDS

During April, 1861, the King's Mountain Guards from York County became Company F, 5th South Carolina Infantry Regiment. Ordered to Virginia the regiment fought at First Manassas under D.R. Jones, then was attached to General R.H. Anderson's, M. Jenkins', and Bratton's Brigade. It participated in the campaigns of the Army of Northern Virginia from Williamsburg to Fredericksburg, served in Longstreet's Suffolk expedition, and was with D.H. Hill in North Carolina. After fighting at Knoxville it returned to Virginia and was prominent in the battles at The Wilderness, Spotsylvania, and Cold Harbor, in the trenches of Petersburg, and around Appomattox. The company surrendered on April 9, 1865, with one first lieutenant, two sergeants, two corporals, and 22 privates. Third Sergeant John Knox then brought the colors home. The hand-painted silk flag, with a scene of King's Mountain on the reverse side, measures 36 inches on the staff and 39 inches on the fly. The lettering is embroidered and its gold thread fringe is 3 inches wide. It now rests at the Confederate Relic Room and Museum at Columbia.

SHEA'S -VERNON'S TEXAS BATTERY

Daniel D. Shea's Battery was organized with men from Bee County and was often called the Van Dorn Guards. Late in 1861, the unit became part of Shea's Texas Artillery Battalion and Captain J.A. Vernon took command. During the summer of 1862, Shea's Battalion was consolidated with the 8th Texas Infantry Battalion to form the 8th Texas Infantry Regiment which contained one cavalry, four infantry, and five artillery companies. Attached to the Trans-Mississippi Department, the cavalry and infantry companies fought primarily in Texas, but did see action at Mansfield and Pleasant Hill in Louisiana. The artillery companies, including the Van Dorn Guards, were stationed along the Texas coast. After fighting at Lavaca, the battery served at Galveston until the end of the war. Their silk battle flag measures 36 inches by 46 inches and was never lost or surrendered. It is now at The Museum of the Confederacy.

REGIMENTAL FLAGS EASTERN THEATRE

The red flag with the blue cross adopted by the Army of Northern Virginia was issued in specified sizes for the different branches of the army: Infantry being 48 inches square, Artillery being 36 inches square, and Cavalry being 30 inches square. The first flag issued during November, 1861, contained twelve gold or white stars and were made of silk by a group of ladies in Richmond. They were presented by General Beauregard in person with the expressed hope and confidence that they would become the emblem of honor and victory. In 1862, the Quartermaster Department supplied the army with machine-sewn flags made of English bunting. These contained thirteen white stars bunched towards the center star and were bordred in orange. However, in time the orange border was replaced with one of white. During 1864 and 1865, flags were issued with larger stars that were spread more evenly on the cross. Many had unit designations painted or sewn on the field of the flag, but later the unit designation was painted in yellow on the blue cross above and below the center star. These flags also contained battle honors that indicated the unit had participated in a particular engagement in a military manner. They were stenciled in dark blue or black colors on the red field by the Quartermaster Department. A few commands applied their battle honors with stylized

block letters which were usually painted in white, but a small number were in yellow.

Units serving in the Department of South Carolina, Georgia, and Florida carried a square flag similar to the one in Virginia. Also issued in specified sizes, they were distributed after September 24, 1862, when General Beauregard took command of the department. He replaced the State flags and company colors with battle flags of the St. Andrew's cross pattern. The main difference in these flags and those in Virginia was the method by which they were attached to the flag-staff. The Virginia flags were tied to the staff through eyelets and those used by the department were secured by a sleeve, which was blue for infantry and red for artillery. They contained thirteen evenly spaced stars, were made of bunting, but few had unit designations or battle honors.

General P. G. T. Beauregard

The Quartermaster Department did a relatively good job in supplying the eastern armies with uniform battle flags. Army of Northern Virginia flags were manufactured in Richmond and the Department of South Carolina, Georgia, and Florida flags were made in Charleston. The Quartermaster officials had many problems with production and in the management of field transportation, but various units, and at times complete divisions, received their flags when ordered or needed.

EIGHTH REGIMENT VIRGINIA INFANTRY

The 8th Virginia Regiment, organized at Leesburg, Virginia, in May, 1861, was also called the "Old Bloody Eighth," and from time to time, "The Berkeley Regiment" because its colonel, lieutenant colonel, major, and one captain were the four Berkeley brothers. It served in the Army of Northern Virginia assigned to General Gracie's, Pickett's, and R.B. Garnett's Brigade. The unit was involved in may battles from First Manassas to Gettysburg where it lost about ninety percent of the 193 men engaged. Later it was attached to the Department of Richmond, fought at Drewry's Bluff and Cold Harbor, then took its palce in the Petersburg trenches. Only one surgeon and 11 privates surrendered at Appomattox. Their silk battle flag was issued early in the war and measures 47 inches on the hoist and 50 inches on the fly. The unit designation and battle honors are painted only on the obverse side. Its red field faded to white, the colors of the 8th Infantry are now at The Museum of the Confederacy.

FOURTH TEXAS INFANTRY REGIMENT

During November, 1861, Miss Lula Wigfall presented this silk flag to Colonel John B. Hood, commander of the 4th Texas Infantry. The thirteen stars and field of the flag were made from her mother's wedding dress. Engraved on the metal spear which capped the flag-staff, was the motto, "Fear not, for I am with thee, Say to the North, give up and the South, keep not back." The unit moved to Virginia, became part of Hood's Texas Brigade, and participated in the campaigns of the Army of Northern Virginia from Seven Pines to Appomattox except when it was with Longstreet at Suffolk, Chickamauga, and Knoxville. Color-Sergeant E.M. Francis carried the flag through the first four engagements, but fell wounded at Second Manassas. It was at this battle that the spearhead was struck by a minie ball. At Sharpsburg, the 4th lost fifty-four percent of the 200 engaged and on October 7, 1862, Captain Stephen H. Darden of Company A returned to Texas with the flag. It measures 47 inches by 47 inches and is now at the United Daughters of the Confederacy Museum at Austin.

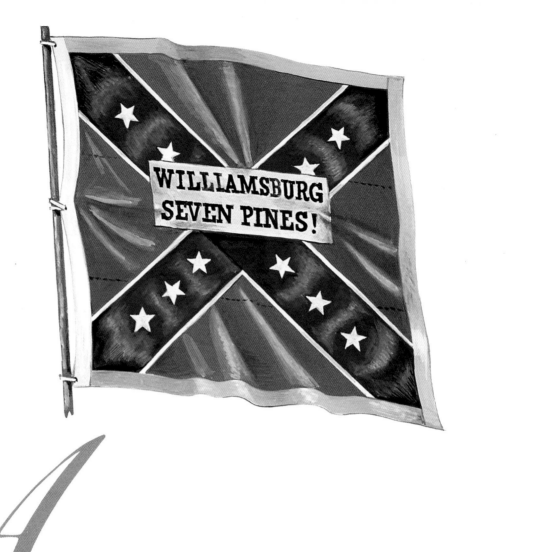

ARMY OF NORTHERN VIRGINIA BATTLE FLAG

UNIDENTIFIED

After the Battle of Gettysburg, Colonel W.G. Veazey of the 16th Vermont Infantry reported: "The two (colors) brought in were the second Florida and the Eighth Virginia. The former had inscribed upon it "Williamsburg" and "Seven Pines." Colonel David Long, commanding General Perry's Brigade at Gettysburg, also reported: "... with infantry on both flanks and in front artillery playing upon us with grape and canister, was certain annihilation. To advance was only to hasten that result, and, therefore, I ordered a retreat, which, however, was not in time to save a large number of the Second Florida Infantry, together with their colors, from being cut off and captured by the flanking force on the left ... " Because this flag lacks a unit designation, it cannot be definitely identified as the colors of the 2nd Florida. It is made of bunting and cotton, measures 49 inches by 49 inches, and the battle honors are painted on cotton strips which are sewn on both sides. The flag is now in a private collection.

FIFTH FLORIDA INFANTRY REGIMENT

The 5th Florida Regiment was organized during the spring of 1861 at Tallahassee, Florida. Ordered to Virginia, it served under Generals Pryor, E.A. Perry, and Finegan, Army of Northern Virginia. At Sharpsburg, five color bearers were shot down. When the order came to fall back, the colors fell again and an officer retrieved the flag under a shower of bullets. At Gettysburg, the flag of the 5th was the only regiment to retain its colors in the Florida Brigade. The reason they were not captured on July 3, 1863, was because Captain Junius L. Taylor of Company K leaped forward as the color bearer fell dead and from his hand tore the flag from its staff and brought it off the field. Colonel Thompson B. Lamar, commander of the 5th, turned the flag over to the State of Florida before he was killed on August 30, 1864, at Petersburg. Their flag, issued during the early summer of 1862, measures 47 inches by 47 inches and is made of bunting and cotton. The unit designation of white fabric was sewn on its field. Never lost or surrendered, it now rests at the Florida State Museum at Tallahassee.

FIRST REGIMENT
VIRGINIA INFANTRY

Organized at Richmond, Virginia, during May, 1861, the 1st Virginia Regiment contained seven companies from Richmond and one from Washington, D.C. It fought at First Manassas under General Longstreet, then served in General A.P. Hill's, Kemper's, and W.R. Terry's Brigade, Army of Northern Virginia. The unit participated in the campaigns of the army from Williamsburg to Gettysburg except when it was with Longstreet at Suffolk. Later it was involved in the capture of Plymouth, the conflicts at Drewry's Bluff and Cold Harbor, the Petersburg siege, and the Appomattox Campaign. The 1st lost more than half of the 209 engaged at Gettysburg. Here their battle flag lay among the dead and dying on Cemetery Ridge. The color guard was dead and the Color-Sergeant lost his arm. A member of the 82nd New York Infantry then captured the colors. Only 17 men surrendered on April 9, 1865. The bunting and cotton flag measures 45 inches by 45 inches and the unit designation is painted. It survives at The Museum of the Confederacy.

SIXTH REGIMENT VIRGINIA INFANTRY

The 6th Regiment was organized at Norfolk, Virginia, on May 13, 1861. During June, 1862, it was placed in General W. Mahone's Brigade with 673 officers and men. Later the unit was under the command of General D.A. Weisiger. It participated in the campaigns of the Army of Northern Virginia from the Seven Days' Battles to Cold Harbor, then saw action in the Petersburg trenches and around Appomattox. On July 30, 1864, after the Petersburg mine explosion, the Confederates turned back the Federal advance. In this fight, there were rapid volleys and counterattacks by General Malone's Division and the 6th Virginia captured the colors of the 11th New Hampshire Regiment and the 45th Pennsylvania Infantry captured this flag from the 6th. The next day the lines were reestablished. Their battle flag measures 47 inches by 47 inches and is made of bunting and cotton. The unit designation of black silk is sewn on its red field. It survives at The Museum of the Confederacy.

THIRTY-SEVENTH NORTH CAROLINA INFANTRY REGIMENT

Organized by Colonel Charles C. Lee in November, 1861, the 37th Regiment assembled at High Point, North Carolina. After fighting at New Bern, the unit moved to Virginia and served in General Branch's and Lane's Brigade. It participated in the campaigns of the Army of Northern Virginia from the Seven Days' Battles to Cold Harbor, then continued the fight in the trenches of Petersburg and around Appomattox. The regiment reported 125 casualties during the Seven Days' Battles, 81 at Second Manassas, 23 at Ox Hil, 93 at Fredericksburg, 235 at Chancellorsville, and 95 at Spotsylvania. After long and hard service their battle flag was captured at Petersburg on April 2, 1865, by the 37th Massachusetts Regiment. It is a unique flag because of its painted, stylized battle honors and on the reverse side are five additional honors: Manassas Junction, Sharpsburg, Mechanicsville, Harper's Ferry, and Sheperdstown. The bunting and cotton flag measures 48 1/2 inches by 48 inches and is now on display at the Lee Chapel Museum, Washington and Lee University, Lexington, Virginia.

FORTY-NINTH GEORGIA INFANTRY REGIMENT

The 49th Georgia was organized in November, 1861, and was soon ordered to Virginia. Here it was attached to General J.R. Anderson's, then E.L. Thomas' Brigade, Army of Northern Virginia. The regiment reported 68 casualties at Second Manassas and 61 at Fredericksburg. Before the Battle of Chancellorsville, April 29, 1863, the unit totalled 398 men, but lost 118 from sickness and fatigue by the time it entered the conflict. Of the 280 who saw action, thirteen percent were disabled. After the battle, this was one of the flags issued with battle honors by the Quartermaster Department to A.P. Hill's Division. It was carried at Gettysburg where the unit lost twenty-five percent of the 329 engaged, during The Wilderness Campaign, and in the long continuous fight against Grant around Petersburg. On April 9, 1865, at Appomattox Courthouse, the 49th Regiment surrendered eight officers, 103 men, and its battle flag. Made of bunting and cotton and measuring 45 inches by 46 inches, it is now on display in the rotunda of the Georgia State Capitol in Atlanta.

TENTH LOUISIANA INFANTRY REGIMENT

Companies that made up the 10th Regiment assembled at Camp Moore, Louisiana, during June and July, 1861. Wearing zouave uniforms, the regiment was composed of many foreigners, including Greeks, Italians, and Spaniards. It soon moved to Virginia, joined the Army of Northern Virginia, and served under Generals McLaws, Semmes, Starke, Nicholls, Iverson, Stafford, and York. At Malvern Hill, it lost twenty-seven percent of the 318 engaged and more than forty-five percent of the 226 at Gettysburg. After the battle this flag was one of those issued with battle honors to Edward Johnson's Division by the Quartermaster Department. During August, 1863, the regiment contained 16 officers and 93 men and in the fight at Cold Harbor, June 3, 1864, lost their battle flag to the 11th Connecticut Infantry Regiment. It then fought with Early in the Shenandoah Valley and surrendered only four officers and 13 men at Appomattox. Its flag, measuring 48 inches on the staff and 46 inches on the fly and made of bunting and cotton, is now in the collections of the Confederate Memorial Hall at New Orleans.

THIRD ARKANSAS INFANTRY REGIMENT

Companies of the 3rd Arkansas assembled at Lynchburg, Virginia, in June, 1861. After serving in western Virginia it was assigned to General J.G. Walker's, J.B. Robertson's, and J. Gregg's command and was part of Hood's Texas Brigade. The unit participated in many conflicts of the Army of Northern Virginia from the Seven Days' Battles to Appomattox except when it was with Longstreet at Suffolk, Chickamauga, and Knoxville. When the regiment surrendered on April 9, 1865, there was a piece of paper pasted to the staff of its battle flag. It said, "Mr. Yankee, you will please return this Flag staff and shoulder belt to the 9th Maine, was captured at St. [sic-Ft.] Gilmore on the 29th October [sic-September] 1864 by the 3rd Forks [sic-Arks] Regt. Vols." The note was signed "Big Rebel." Their flag, issued late in the war, was made of bunting and cotton and measures 51 1/2 inches by 50 inches. It is now on display at the Lee Chapel Museum, Washington and Lee University, Lexington, Virginia.

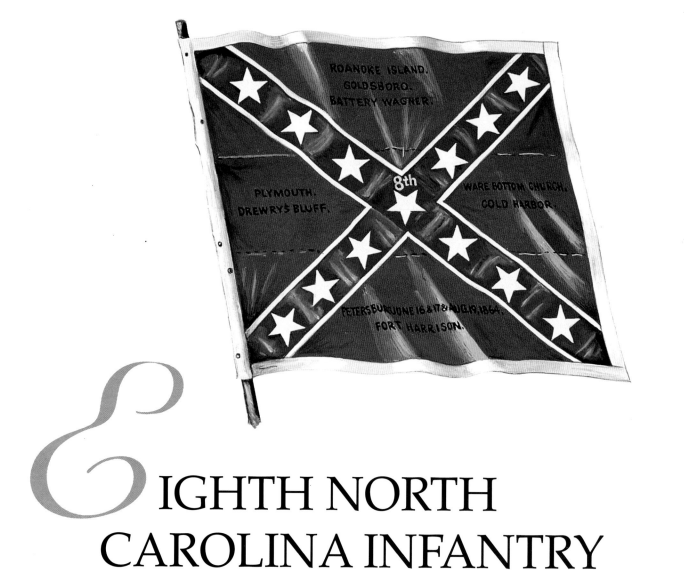

EIGHTH NORTH CAROLINA INFANTRY REGIMENT STATE TROOPS

After being captured at Roanoke Island in February, 1862, the men of the 8th North Carolina were exchanged and reorganized at Camp Mangum during September. Assigned to General T.L. Clingman's Brigade, the unit fought in North and South Carolina, joined the Army of Northern Virginia, and ended the war in North Carolina with the Army of Tennessee. In the conflict at Plymouth, the 8th lost thirty-two percent of its force and color bearer F. J. Perkins was killed. At Fort Harrison, its casualites were eighty-five percent of the 175 engaged. Color bearer J.R. Barnhardt found that he could not escape capture and tore the old flag, that had seen so much service, to pieces to keep it from falling into the hands of the enemy. During October or November, 1864, this flag was issued with battle honors by the Quartermaster Department and was carried by J.V. Fisher until the end of the war. When news came that Johnston had surrendered he saved the flag from being cut up for war mementoes and took it home. The colors of the 8th are made of bunting and cotton and measures 46 1/2 inches on the staff and 51 inches on the fly. It is now in a private collection.

SIXTEENTH SOUTH CAROLINA INFANTRY REGIMENT

Recruited in Greenville County, the 16th South Carolina Infantry was organized and mustered into Confederate service in December, 1861. It moved to Charleston and for a time was stationed at Adams Run under General Hagood. During December, 1862, the unit was ordered to Wilmington, North Carolina, and in May, 1863, to Jackson, Mississippi, where it was assigned to General Gist's Brigade in the Department of Mississippi and East Louisiana. After sharing in the defense of Jackson, it was stationed at Rome, Georgia, during the Chickamauga Campaign. Later the regiment joined the Army of Tennessee and ended the war in North Carolina. Their battle flag is of the pattern issued by the Department of South Carolina, Georgia, and Florida. It measures 46 inches on the staff and 48 inches on the fly, is made of cotton and bunting, and the unit designation is painted on cotton strips and sewn on its field. The flag is now at the Confederate Relic Room and Museum at Columbia.

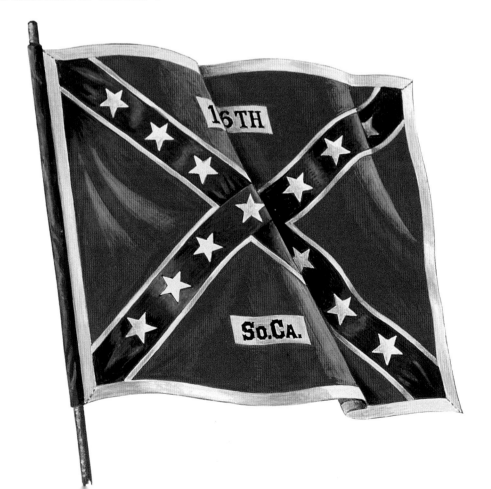

REGIMENTAL FLAGS WESTERN THEATRE

Because of the similarity between the "Stars and Bars" and the "Stars and Stripes," commanders in the western theatre adopted their own battle flags. General Bragg's Corps was issued a square red flag with a blue St. Andrew's cross with twelve six-pioonted stars and a pink border. These flags were made in New Orleans and later a second group was ordered of the same pattern, but its shape was rectangular. Leonidas Polk's Corps used a blue rectangular flag with a red St. George's cross that contained eleven stars, and General Hardee's forces carried a blue flag with a white border and a white round or oval disk in the center. Earl Van Dorn's command adopted a red flag bordered in yellow or white with thirteen white stars and a crescent. General John P. McCown's Division of Kirby Smith's Department of East Tennesee (Army of Kentucky) carried a blue flag with a white St. Andrew's cross and no stars. Missouri troops were issued a blue oblong flag bordered in red with a white Latin cross near its hoist. These flags were also manufactured in New Orleans. The flag of the Department of Alabama, Mississippi, and East Louisiana was of the Virginia pattern but contained twelve stars and no border. Other units in the west also carried flags of the St. Andrew's cross pattern, but in a few cases the colors were reversed.

General Joseph E. Johnston

When many of these commands, or elements thereof, became part of the Army of Tennessee, they brought their battle flags with them. During November, 1863, General Joseph E. Johnston was placed in command of the army and wanted to standardize the colors as it was done for the Army of Northern Virginia. In the spring of 1864 a new battle flag was issued. It was rectangular in shape and contained a blue St. Andrew's cross with thirteen white stars upon a red field. Generals Hardee and Hood issued orders that the flags will have inscribed on them the number of the regiment and the State to which it belongs. General Hood also stated that "But one stand of colors will be used by any regiment in time of battle."

However, Johnston's efforts to secure a uniform battle flag was not achieved. Various commands wanted to keep their original patterns and when the Army of Tennessee surrendered in April, 1865, national flags, the Hardee battle flag, the flag adopted by the Department of Alabama, Mississippi, and East Louisiana, and Johnston's Army of Tennessee flag were all in use. Many contained battle honors which were the names of the engagements they had participated in, and a few displayed crossed cannon barrels (often inverted) indicating the capture of Federal artillery.

EIGHTH TEXAS CAVALRY REGIMENT

The 8th Texas Cavalry, usually known as Terry's Texas Rangers, was organized by Ben Franklin Terry and Thomas B. Lubbock. It was formed with 1170 men at Houston, Texas, on September 9, 1861. Its members enlisted for the "duration of the war" and were the "best Texas had to offer." Each man furnished his own equipment and arms, most were in their teens and early twenties, and no one paid much attention to rank. It was one of the hardest fighting units in the war and served under Generals Wheeler, Wharton, and T. Harrison. The Rangers fought at Shiloh, Murfreesboro, and Chickamauga, then saw action in the Knoxville and Atlanta Campaigns. Later it took an active part in the defense of Savannah and the campaign of the Carolinas. About 30 men surrendered with the Army of Tennessee. This Bonnie Blue Flag, part of the collections of the Chicago Historical Society, was carried by the regiment early in the war. It measures 23 1/2 inches by 32 inches, is made of bunting, and the lettering is painted.

FIRST TENNESSEE INFANTRY REGIMENT VOLUNTEERS

During May, 1861, the 1st Tennessee Regiment Volunteers was organized at Nashville, Tennessee. It was ordered to Virginia, saw action in Lee's Cheat Mountain Campaign, served under T.J. Jackson, then in February, 1862, returned to Tennessee. After fighting at Shiloh and Perryville the unit was attached to General Maney's and Palmer's Brigade, Army of Tennessee, and during December, 1862, consolidated with the 27th Tennessee Regiment. It participated in the campaigns of the army from Murfreesboro to Atlanta, endured Hood's Tennessee operations, and fought in North Carolina. The 1st/27th sustained 83 casualties at Murfreesboro and 89 at Chickamauga, and in December, 1863, totalled 456 men and 290 arms. About 125 effectives surrendered on April 26, 1865. This Polk pattern flag was issued after the Battle of Perryville. It measures 28 inches on the staff and 46 inches on the fly and the unit designation is painted on a cotton strip which was sewn to the silk flag. The colors of the 1st now rests at the Tennessee State Museum at Nashville.

TWENTY-SECOND ALABAMA INFANTRY REGIMENT

The 22nd Alabama Infantry completed its organization at Montgomery, Alabama, in November, 1861. After serving at Mobile it fought at Shiloh and saw action in the Kentucky Campaign. Later it was assigned to General Deas', G.D. Johnston's, and Brantley's Brigade, Army of Tennessee. The unit served with the army from Murfreesboro to Atlanta, was part of Hood's winter operations in Tennessee, and surrendered in North Carolina. It sustained 94 casualties at Murfreesboro and lost fifty-three percent of the 371 engaged at Chickamauga. Here one man was killed and two were wounded carrying this flag. It was captured on September 20, 1863, by the 121st Ohio Regiment and because of the confusion the 22nd fell back. Twice the regiment attempted to recover its ground and flag, but the storm of grape and canister were too much. This variation of the Polk battle flag is made of cotton and measures 41 1/2 inches on the staff and 54 1/2 inches on the fly. The fringe is silk and the unit designation and battle honors were embroidered. It is part of the collections of the Alabama Department of Archives and History at Montgomery.

THIRTIETH ARKANSAS INFANTRY REGIMENT

This unit completed its organization at Little Rock, Arkansas, during the late summer of 1861 using the 11th Arkansas Battalion as its nucleus. It was designated the 30th Regiment; however, in January or February, 1863, the unit was redesignated the 25th because of irregularities in the Arkansas numbering sequence. After serving in the Army of Kentucky it was assigned to General McNair's and D.H. Reynold's Brigade, Army of Tennessee. At the Battle of Murfreesboro it had seven company commanders and the color bearer cut down. Later in the day (December 31, 1862), a second color bearer had his hand shot off and the flag was lost in a cedar break to the 2nd Ohio Infantry Regiment. The unit then fought at Jackson and with the army from Chickamauga to Bentonville. Their cotton battle flag is of the pattern adopted by the Department of East Tennessee. It measures 40 inches by 46 inches, and the unit designation and battle honors were painted in outline letters and numbers. It is now in the collections of The Old State House at Little Rock.

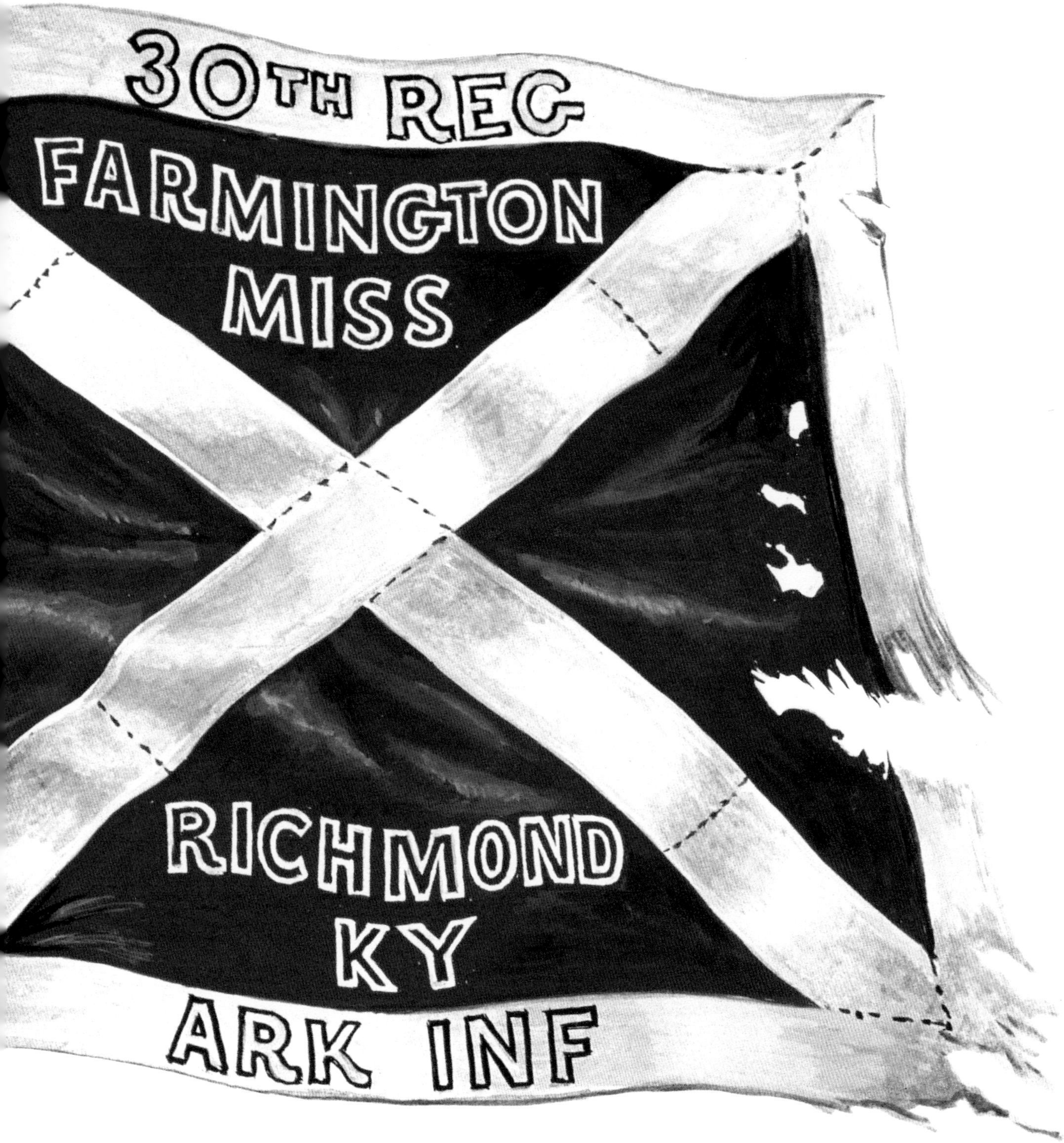
30TH REG
FARMINGTON
MISS
RICHMOND
KY
ARK INF

SEVENTH MISSISSIPPI INFANTRY REGIMENT

Organized at Corinth, Mississippi, in April, 1861, the 7th Regiment was mustered into Confederate service with 911 men. It served on the Mississippi coast at Bay St. Louis, joined the Army of the Mississippi, saw action in the Kentucky Campaign, then was assigned to General J.R. Anderson's, Tucker's, and Sharp's Brigade, Army of Tennessee. The unit participated in many conflicts of the army from Murfreesboro to Atlanta, marched with Hood to Tennessee, and fought in North Carolina. It reported 20 casualties at Munfordville, 113 at Murfreesboro, and 75 at Chickamauga. The regiment was briefley consolidated with the 9th Mississippi Infantry in December, 1863, and this command totalled 468 men and 252 arms. On April 26, 1865, it surrendered with 10 officers and 64 men. Their battle flag was designed by General Beauregard and was one of those first issued to General Bragg's forces. It is made of cotton with silk stars and a serge border, and measures 48 1/2 inches on the staff and 42 1/2 inches on the fly. The colors of the 7th Regiment are now at the Mississippi State Historical Museum at Jackson.

FIFTY-SEVENTH GEORGIA INFANTRY REGIMENT

The 57th Georgia was organized during the spring of 1862 with men from Troup, Peach, Montgomery, and Oconee counties. It served in East Tennessee and Kentucky, then moved to Mississippi where it was attached to Colonel T.H. Taylor's Brigade in the Department of Mississippi and East Louisiana. The unit fought at Champion's Hill and was captured on July 4, 1863, at Vicksburg. Exchanged and rearmed, it was assigned to General Mercer's and J.A. Smith's Brigade, and saw action in various engagements from Resaca to Bentonville. During the Atlanta Campaign, July 20 to September 1, 1864, it reported 54 casualties and that December totalled 120 effectives. Only a remnant surrendered with the Army of Tennessee. The battle flag of the 57th is of the second set of flags designed and ordered during the spring of 1862 by General Beauregard and issued to General Bragg's troops. It measures 42 1/2 inches by 73 1/2 inches, is made of cotton, and the stars and border are silk. The flag is now in the collections of The Museum of the Confederacy.

FIFTEENTH ARKANSAS INFANTRY REGIMENT

McRae's - Hobb's - Boone's

Using McRae's 3rd Arkansas Battalion of eight companies as its nucleus, the 15th Regiment was formed in December, 1861. The unit was also call the 21st or Northwest Regiment. It served in the Trans-Mississippi Department, then moved east of the Mississippi River. Here the regiment was attached to General M.E. Green's and Colonel T.P. Doctery's Brigade in the Department of Mississippi and East Louisiana. This flag was probably presented to the command during October or November, 1862. In the fight at Port Gibson, May 1, 1863, it sustained 82 casualites and lost its color bearer and battle flag to the 18th Indiana Infantry Regmient. Later the 15th became part of the garrison captured at Vicksburg on July 4th. When the men were exchanged the unit was not reorganized. Their Van Dorn pattern flag measures 46 inches on the staff and 65 inches on the fly and is made of bunting. The stars, unit designation, and battle honors are cotton, and the crescent, border, and fringe are silk. It is now at The Old State House in Little Rock.

*F*IRST MISSOURI CAVALRY REGIMENT

Men from the Missouri State Guard formed the 1st Missouri Cavalry Regiment during the summer of 1861. It fought at Elkhorn Tavern, then moved east of the Mississippi River and was dismounted. Serving in General M.E. Green's Brigade, Department of Mississippi and East Louisiana, the unit took an active part in the fight at Big Black River Bridge. Here on May 17, 1863, its battle flag was captured by the 11th Wisconsin Infantry. On July 4th the regiment was captured at Vicksburg. After being exchanged and reorganized it was consolidated with the 3rd (Samuel's) Missouri Cavalry Battalion. Assigned to General Cockrell's Brigade, Army of Tennessee, this command, serving as infantry, lost 25 killed, 80 wounded, and 3 missing during the Atlanta Campaign. It went on to fight with Hood in Tennessee and ended the war at Mobile. Their "Missouri Battle Flag" measures 36 inches on the staff and 51 inches on the fly, is made of cotton, and the Latin cross is sewn on its field. It is now at the State Capital Museum, Jefferson City, Missouri.

$\mathcal{E}$IGHTEENTH ALABAMA INFANTRY REGIMENT

The 18th Infantry Regiment completed its organization in September, 1861, at Auburn, Alabama. It was attached to the Department of Alabama and West Florida, then during March, 1862, moved to Tennessee. Assigned to J.K. Jackson's Brigade, the unit took an active part in the fight at Shiloh. After serving at Mobile it was attached to General Clayton's and Holtzclaw's Brigade and fought with the Army of Tennessee from Chickamauga to Nashville. In January, 1865, the unit returned to Mobile. The regiment totalled 858 men in January, 1862, and lost 100 at Shiloh and fifty-six percent of the 527 engaged at Chickamauga. In the Battle of Missionary Ridge on November 25, 1863, the 18th lost its battle flag to the 13th Illinois Regiment. The Hardee pattern flag measures 34 inches on the staff and 37 1/2 on the fly and is made of wool and cotton. The unit designation is painted. It is now part of the collections of the Alabama Department of Archives and History at Montgomery.

THIRD CONFEDERATE INFANTRY REGIMENT

With two companies from Mississippi and eight from Arkansas, the 3rd Confederate Regiment was organized during Janaury, 1862. It served in General Wood's, L.E. Polk's, and Govan's Brigade, Army of Tennessee. From February, 1863, to April, 1864, it was consolidated with the 5th (Smith's) Confederate Regiment and this command sustained many casualties at Chickamauga and in December, 1863, totalled 338 men and 232 arms. During July, 1864, the 3rd had only 62 men present for duty. At the Battle of Jonesboro on September 1st, about eight o'clock in the evening, its battle flag was captured by the 113th Ohio Infantry. The small unit continued the fight with Hood in Tennessee and surrendered in North Carolina. This Hardee pattern flag, which Cleburne's Division was permitted to retain after Johnston had issued new flags of the St. Andrew's cross design, is made of cotton and measures 30 inches by 35 1/2 inches. The unit designation, crossed cannon barrels, and battle honors are painted. It is now at the Alabama Department of Archives and History at Montgomery.

FOURTH MISSISSIPPI INFANTRY REGIMENT

With 787 officers and men the 4th Mississippi Regiment was organized at Grenada, Mississippi, in April 1861. It moved to Tennessee where a detachment was captured at Fort Henry and the regiment at Fort Donelson. After being exchanged the unit served in the Department of Mississippi and East Louisiana and was again captured at Vicksburg. Exchanged and rearmed it was assigned to General Baldwin's and Sear's Brigade, Army of Tennessee. The 4th saw action in the Atlanta Campaign, fought with Hood in Tennessee, and ended the war defending Mobile. In the Confederate works at Nashville it lost its battle flag on December 16, 1864, to Lieutenant T.P. Gere of the 5th Minnesota Infantry Regiment. Of course, Lieutenant Gere was awarded the Medal of Honor. The flag is of the Department of Alabama, Mississippi, and East Louisiana pattern and is hand-stitched with appliqued stars, unit designation, and battle honors. The wool bunting flag measures 46 inches on the staff and 52 inches on the fly and survives at the Mississippi State Historical Museum.

SIXTH KENTUCKY INFANTRY REGIMENT

The 6th Kentucky Regiment was organized at Cave City, Kentucky, in November, 1861, and includes Cofer's 1st Kentucky Infantry Battalion. It became part of the Orphan Brigade or Louisville Legion and during the war served under the command of Generals Hanson, Helm, and J.H. Lewis. The unit lost 108 men at Shiloh, 18 at Baton Rouge, and seventeen percent of the 269 at Murfreesboro. In the fight at Chickamauga 220 saw action and in December, 1863, there were 263 present for duty. At Jonesboro on September 1, 1864, its battle flag and most of the regiment were captured by the 10th Michigan Regiment in a hard fight. Later the 6th was reorganized and mounted, participated in the defense of Savannah and the North Carolina Campaign, and surrendered with the Army of Tennessee on April 26, 1865. Their Johnston pattern flag measures 36 1/2 inches by 51 inches and is made of bunting and cotton. The unit designation, crossed inverted cannon barrels, and battle honors were painted. It survives at the Kentucky Historical Society in Frankfort.

BATTLE FLAG OF GENERAL SHELBY'S BRIGADE

Joseph O. Shelby was active in almost every campaign of the war west of the Mississippi river. He saw action at Carthage, Wilson's Creek, Lexington, Elkhorn Tavern, Prairie Grove, Helena, Camden, and in Price's Missouri Operations. Late in the war his Iron Brigade included the 5th, 11th, and 12th Regiments and the 1st and A.W. Slayback's Battalions of Missouri Cavalry, and R.A. Collins' Missouri Battery. After the Army of the Trans-Mississippi Department was surrendered, Shelby's command rode through Texas and crossed the Rio Grande into Mexico. It is said that his men carried along their bullet-ridden battle flags and buried them along the bank before crossing the river. However, this flag was retrieved by one of his men. It is made of silk, measures 57 inches on the staff and 54 1/2 inches on the fly, and is now part of the collections of the Oklahoma Historical Society in Oklahoma City.

THIRD TEXAS INFANTRY REGIMENT

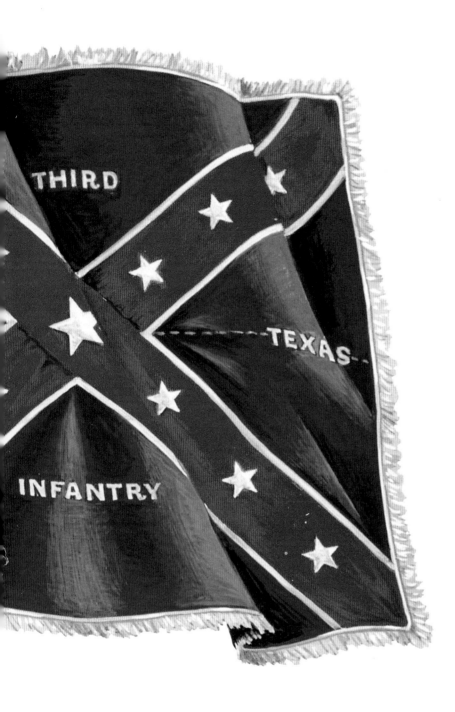

The 3rd Texas Infantry was organized during the fall of 1861 by Colonel Philip N. Lickett. Some of its members were recruited at San Antonio and Austin. It never left the State of Texas, but served along the coast at various points. The unit or detachments of it were stationed at Galveston, Velasco, Houston, Brownsville, Sabine Pass, and other locations. During October, 1864, it totalled 648 officers and men. Because the regiment never saw action, morale deteriorated during the later part of the war. This flag was made by a group of ladies from Galveston and presented to the 3rd Regiment. The color reversal on the flag is typical of the flags carried in western Louisiana and Texas from late 1863 to the close of the war. It is made of silk and the unit designation and stars are embroidered in silver wire thread. It measures 45 inches on the staff and 48 1/2 on the fly. The unit disbanded prior to the surrender in June, 1865, and its colors are now at the United Daughters of the Confederacy Museum in Austin.

CHOCTAW BATTLE FLAG

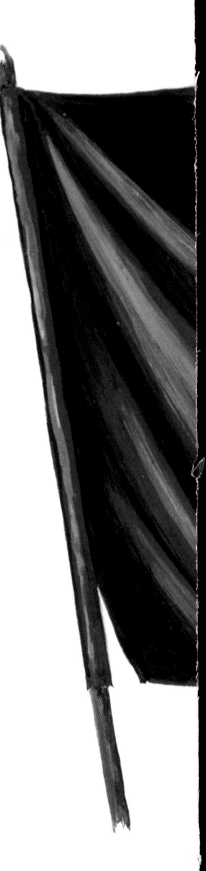

About 2,000 Choctaw Indians served in the Confederate army. They formed the 1st and 3rd Regiments and the 1st War Regiment of Choctaw Cavalry, and six companies became part of the 1st Choctaw and Chickasaw Mounted Rifles. They were all assigned to the Department of the Indian Territory (area now in the State of Oklahoma, excluding the panhandle which was known as the Public Land Strip), Trans-Mississippi Department. It is unclear as to which of these units carried this battle flag that is now on display at the Oklahoma Historical Society in Oklahoma City. It measures 40 inches on the staff and 62 inches on the fly, is made of blue and red cotton, but the white circle, bow, arrows, and tomahawk are silk. The flag contains the emblem used by the tribe. The bow is not strung, indicating that the Choctaw were a peaceful people, but the arrows and tomahawk signified they were always ready to defend themselves.

CREDITS

Page 2-3   Lee recumbent statue in Lee Chapel at Washington & Lee University by William Strode.

Page 9-10   Illustrations by Frank Leslie.

Page 13   W. Porcher Miles — South Carolina Library, The University of South Carolina, Columbia, S.C.

Page 29   Hetty Cary, 29; Jennie Cary, 30; Connie Cary, 31 — Bill Turner, La Plata, Maryland.

Page 35   General Thomas J. "Stonewall" Jackson — Author's collection.

Page 43   Turner Ashby — Author's collection.

Page 55   Captain James J. White — Duncan McConnell Photography Collection, The University Library, Washington and Lee University, Lexington, Virginia.

Page 72   General P.G.T. Beauregard — Bill Turner, La Plata, Maryland.

Page 88   General Joseph E. Johnston — Bill Turner, La Plata, Maryland.

Page One   The battle flag of the 38th Alabama was captured at Resaca, Georgia, May 15, 1864, by the 27th Indiana Infantry Regiment. The inverted cannon barrels and lettering were sewn on the bunting flag and is now part of the collections of the Alabama Department of Archives and History, Montgomery, Alabama.

Page Four   Flag of the 36th Virginia captured at the Third Battle of Winchester, September 19, 1864, by the 6th New York Cavalry Regiment. The Virginia seal, unit designation, and battle honors were hand-painted. It is now at the Museum of the Confederacy, Richmond, Virginia.

BIBLIOGRAPHY

Amann, William. *Personnel of the Civil War*. Volume I, The Confederate Armies. New York: Thomas Yoseloff, 1961.

Bean, W.G. *The Liberty Hall Volunteers*. Charlottesville: The University Press of Virginia, 1964.

Confederate Veteran, The. 40 vols., January, 1893 - December, 1932. Nashville, Tenessee. 1893-1932. (Founded by S.A. Cunningham)

Crute, Joseph H., Jr. *Confederate Staff Officers 1861-1865*. Powhatan, Virginia: Derwent Books, 1982.

Crute, Joseph H., Jr. *Units of the Confederate State Army*. Midlothian, Virginia: Derwent Books, 1987.

Flags of the Confederate Armies, The. *Returned to the Men Who Bore Them by the United States Government, 1905*.

Henderson, Harry McCorry. *Texas in the Confederacy*. San Antonio: The Naylor Company, 1955.

Histories of the Several Regiments and Battalions from North Carolina in the Great War, 1861-1865. 5 vols, Ed. Walter Clark, Raleigh: State of North Carolina, 1901.

Jones, Tom. *Hood's Texas Brigade Sketch Book*. Hillsboro, Texas: Hill College Press, 1988.

Journal of the Congress of the Confederate States of America, 1861–1865. Vol. I-VIII. Washington: United States Printing Office, 1905.

LaBree, Ben. Ed. *The Confederate Soldier in the Civil War 1861-1865*. Louisville, Kentucky: The Courier-Journal Printing Company, 1895.

Loehr, Charles T. *War History of the Old First Virginia Infantry Regiment, Army of Northern Virginia*. 1884. Dayton, Ohio: Morningside Bookshop, 1970.

Madaus, Howard Michael. *The Battle Flags of the Confederate Army of Tennessee*. Milwaukee: Milwaukee Public Museum, 1976.

Manakee, Harold R. *Maryland in the Civil War*. Baltimore, Maryland: Garamond/Pridemark Press, 1969.

Oates, Stephen B. *Confederate Cavalry West of the River*. Austin, Texas: University of Texas Press, 1961.

U.S. War Department. *Official Records of the Union and Confederate Armies in the War of the Rebellion*. 128 parts in 70 vols. Washington, D.C., 1880-1901.

Tennessee Civil War Commission. *Tennesseans in the Civil War*. Nashville,Tennessee, 1964.

United Confederate Veterans. The Flags of the Confederate States of America. Baltimore, Maryland: A. Hoen & Co., 1907.

Wannamaker, W. W. Captain USRN (Ret.) *A Story of American Flags*. The State Printing Company, Columbia, South Carolina, 1971.

BATTLE FLAG INDEX